"BEYOND THEZE WALLZ"
"A POETIC
AUTOBIOGRAPHY"

An insightfully compelling true story about one man's life, welded together by the diversity of experiences uncommon to most men! Centered into the background of twentieth century urban America. It raises genuine questions and evokes the heart and mind of any discerning reader to pause, ponder, gasp, hope and wonder, as the prejudices, and ironies of race, religion, cultural differences, and this world's incessant obsession with vice, folly, power and greed avail themselves upon page after page. Anchored juxtapose these moving episodes are powerful quotations from the leading thinker's, (men and women), iconic figures of old and new, and by far, the greatest gift to us all is the skill, wit and terse with which the author's poetry makes its international debut with one awe-inspiring poem, behind another, behind another, behind another! This book is a must read! "Not just a book, but an amazing living testament!" "A spiritual journey!"
K. B. Akbar

To Mr. Hill,
   A man ~~that~~ became one of the early ~~positive~~ influences in my life because he was my ~~father's~~ dearest friend ~~throughout the~~ years. Thank you so much

"BEYOND THEZE WALLZ"

~~for~~ being the man that you are. God bless you!
   Sincerely,
   K. A.
   01/05/18

"Beyond Theze Wallz"

"A Poetic Autobiography"

K. B. Akbar

Copyrights 2017 K. B. Akbar
Akonelikenone1958@gmail.com

All rights are reserved except for text references. No part of this book may be used or reproduced in any manner whatsoever without prior written consent from the author.

ISBN: 1545462097
ISBN 13: 9781545462096

Table of Contents

Introduction ix
Acknowledgements. .xvii

Chapter 1	"The Awakening"	1
Chapter 2	"Attrtition"	17
Chapter 3	"The Sentence".	37
Chapter 4	"County Jail"	56
Chapter 5	"State Prison".	72
Chapter 6	"PIA and PWC'S"	97
Chapter 7	"The Hypocrazy"	116
Chapter 8	"The Stand".	134
Chapter 9	"Transfer"	159
Chapter 10	"Release in Sight"	177

Epilogue 215
About the Author. 223

INTRODUCTION

WHEN ONE EMBARKS on a task as tedious and arduous as writing a book, especially one that attempts to convey the real dimensions and diversity of life's experiences, so many issues and concerns are raised. The most virtuous stance is one grounded in sheer honesty and truth, yet some of the most remote sensitivities come to mind when enigmatic sentiments and vague thoughts find clarity in the analogy of words. So many of us spend a lifetime without discovering *the real beauty and power of an enlightened pen.*

I thank GOD for the inspiration to write, even in my earliest memories and limited scope. As an adolescent, *I began writing or capturing my thoughts and sentiments as a constructive outlet in diaries and journals.* I soon realized that by transferring my feelings, (sometimes anxieties), from my heart to a piece of paper, I felt relieved and less burdened by its weight or pressure. In High School, History and English Literature were two of my favorite subjects. It was there in my English Literature class that my teacher, (Mrs. Rawls), would introduce me to what became one of my life long loves and passions-*Poetry.*

It was this same teacher that recognized a latent talent and appreciation in me toward this art. In no time I became known as the *"Poet of my Peers",* and Mrs. Rawls invested time outside of my regular classroom hour to nurture this fledgling gift in me. I recall her words verbatim: *"You have a natural talent, cultivate it and save your material for future publication."* I owe so much to this brief yet meaningful encounter, for I have never forgotten her caring words to me. And since age fifteen, I have accumulated volumes of poetry. My writing skills improved with my command of the English language and with the scope of my personal experiences in life.

The courage to share these personal writings with others grew as my parents and siblings, (my initial audience and first loyal fans), nudged me out of our home and into a broader audience. I learned early on also, (like any real novice or accomplished writer can attest to), **that writing materials of some sort must always be accessible,** because the surge of inspiration can leave as quickly as it came, and if some portion of it, (a partial verse, a compelling title, something), is not captured, it may not be retrievable later in its original form. In addition to this, and far more vexing, is the opening of the **writer's Pandora's Box!** It is akin to a razor sharp double edged sword that cuts deeply and permanently.

The deep, in-depth preponderance of life, with of all of its corollary issues and concerns, aside from what I've read and studied, I have been afforded a pool of unique experiences, (Older siblings actively involved in the Black Power movement of the 60's and 70's; Parents born in the Jim Crow era of the South and involved in the Civil Rights movement of the 40's, 50's and 60's; and Grandparents born before the turn of the twentieth century in -this country), **kept me baptized in a rich, first-hand account of what life was and what life is.** So all of this groomed me to think outside the box, and as a result of this, **my consciousness, my thinking**, exceeded my adolescent years. So as I dipped into this deep, cool well of experience to extend a drink to those around me, they rejected it. *I felt alienated and* *alone amongst my peers* because none of them thought or shared the concerns that I did, and because of what became known as my controversial views, expressed openly and boldly when asked about them, I was labeled as ***crazy or militant,*** which is the background for one of my oldest poems, written when I was sixteen years old:

"MAD OUTRAGE"
**When I try to relate to people of my age, they
look at me and say you're in a mad outrage.**

**I'm on a higher plane than most of the others, the
materialistic minds of my sisters and brothers.**

**When I try to relate about the evilness of this land,
the corruption and confusion I can no longer stand!**

**My people I pray that you make it through this stage,
for indeed you're the ones in the "MAD OUTRAGE!"**
KBA

It can be a very lonely place to reach a certain level of awareness that most people around you can't see or relate to. Like a horror movie where there is an imminent, ominous threat to all of us, and everyone else drifted into a deep sleep and you're the only one awake!

"There are few things in the world as
dangerous as sleepwalkers!"

RALPH ELLISON

"Beyond Theze Wallz," "A Poetic Autobiography", really began many years ago. Being involved in writer's guilds and literary circles from the east to the west coast, (The Black Writers Posey in Atlanta with Regina and Ola; The Riverside Renaissance Writers Guild in California), I've had numerous fellow writers demand completed manuscripts long before now. For one reason or another, (lack of copyrights, lifestyle incongruent with that of a writer, procrastination, etc.), I never finished them. In hindsight I realize today that there were still chapters of my life I needed to experience and get through in order for this material to truly be *a timeless work of art.*

Like going to prison, and subsequent parole!

"Prosperity tries the fortunate, adversity the great!"

Pliny the Great

It was in the confines of that ten foot by twelve foot concrete prison cell that I came to terms with my own personal faults and shortcomings and recommitted myself to the daily cultivation of a sound and personable relationship with the **CREATOR OF ALL THINGS!** Gradually the manuscript grew, as did my experiences in this new and bizarre environment! The title of the book: **"Beyond Theze Wallz," "A Poetic Autobiography,"** availed itself early on in my sojourn through the inspiration of poetic verse, which closes out the book in the epilogue. I thought it appropriate not only because of the setting, but also because of this historic fact which transcends race, color, creed, gender, or culture. All of us, in our earliest childhood experiences have to contend with *the walls or barriers* that family values, cultural experiences in our communities, religious beliefs, societal preferences, biasness or prejudices and/or the lack thereof nurture in us. As we mature from adolescence into adulthood, many of these **constrictive walls or barriers, (invisible walls),** hamper us from embracing a broader, **more cosmopolitan attitude in life and in many cases can and have led to bitter, bloody feuds that have lasted for generations.** As an African American boy born in the South, I am oh so familiar with the sullied **barriers or walls of race and class preferences** and therefore, even as a child and well into my adult years, I have spent days and nights studying and pondering the sources and remedies for one of **Mankind's biggest barriers: "Intolerance for one another!"**

> "The worst sin towards our fellows is not to hate them, but to be indifferent to them; that's the essence of inhumanity."
>
> GEORGE BERNARD SHAW

Now, the body, theme or message we hope to convey caused me by far the greatest reflection, apprehension, and required many hours of deliberation over relevant issues and concerns. First, being African American, there are some poems and episodes in this book that relate to our **own odyssey in this country,** and perhaps only African Americans can relate fervently. Yet it is our committed aim to educate others about this and at the same time interject the **universal concepts of Mankind in some poems by speaking to the beauty of humanity and the noble calling** that awaits us all when we shed the kinds of **self-interests that lead to race and class preferences.**

> "A hundred times every day I remind myself that my
> inner and outer life depend on the labors of men,
> living and dead, and that I must exert myself in order
> to give in the same measure as I have been given."
>
> ALBERT EINSTEIN

I, along with other informed African Americans, contend that our struggle in this country is profound and unique, as are present conditions that exist in our communities all across this country today. **By no means can this continual struggle, with its stories of pain, sorrow, joy, happiness, tragedy, grief, victory and triumph be down-played or underscored, and our hope is to extend these excellent examples of strength, hope, perseverance, fortitude and faith to all people, especially African-Americans. For some of us have forgotten the real moral of our own story, and we must never forget!** There are certain poems and episodes in this book that speak of our **past in biting, caustic terms**. They are intended to jolt those of us asleep out of our **stifled slumber**, and also reflect where I was at that period of my own journey.

I, like any of us, had to evolve to this present, broader scope or perspective of things, and as you read each retrospective chapter may you be blessed to evolve to a higher understanding with us. Under no circumstance is it our aspiration to *promote or condone* the tainting, self-destructive sentiments of hate, bitterness, animosity, and resentments. **We pray that the fallacy of those things will be apparent to you as this book is read.** This effort, like any other human endeavor, **shall not be without error or flaw,** though we sought meticulously to perfect it. Should any discerning reader find some insight or any portion of this book beneficial, **then our efforts have not been in vain, and ALL GLORY AND PRAISE BELONGS TO GOD SOLEY!** This book was written with the hope and aim that *all people* will find it entertaining and useful reading, **and it was intended to be useful material for the whole world….**

"MESSAGE TO THE WORLD"

This is to the world, cultures I may never see, a sincere message of love emanating from me.

One solitary soul, cast far into time and space, surrounding by a great many, people nearly every place.

Trapped in my own thoughts of the world's essence, of the sun, moon, stars and Mankind's presence.

Reflections of old, societies before us, what knowledge this holds, if only we all begin to trust.

In the greatest power, filled with peace, order and love, an unmistakable reference to the Omniscient Force Above.

KBA

"I believe that unarmed truth and unconditional love will have the final word."

Rev. Dr. Martin Luther King Jr.

Acknowledgements

To my friend, my mentor, my wise counselor, my father, endeared to all of us his children as **"Bacadee."** A man who in his lifetime achieved far more than average feats, and left a legacy of altruism wherever he went. An excellent example of what courage, conviction, and a determined will can do!

Arthur David Beavers Jr. (08/11/27-05/16/95). *I Miss You!*

To my Mother **"Gloria",** the epitome of true love, femininity and genteelness. A woman whose personal sacrifices for her husband and nine children, and so many others is a living testament to her divinely guided purpose and presence with all of us.

My Queen of Queens: Gloria Shropshire Beavers. *I Love You!*

To each and every one of my siblings, **(Arthur, June, Deborah, Reginald, Gloria, Angela, Andre and Anthony)**….For all of the love, support and encouragement throughout the years! When this brother wandered down dark corridors, they all came every time, with **GOD'S** light held high, to find this one lost sheep, to bring him back within the fold of the flock. *I Honor You!*

To my four beautiful Children, **(Mikal, Hakim, Kenya, And M'shari)**. And my four beautiful Grandchildren, **(Raquel, Akira, Azari and Nazir)**… For the love and inspiration that only children can provide. *I Adore You!*

To so, so many others, that have walked with me along this journey, many of whom makeup the very tapestry of this work. A very special thanks to **Samuel Benjamin Rains, (Complicated Passions)**, for his mentorship and hand in this work, and **Curtis Armstrong,** for your priceless technical support, keen insight and friendship… To two of my lifelong friends and brothers: **Mustafa Muhammad Shabazz,** a life soldier placed on my path twenty years ago, and a main character in my life and in this work, and **Terry Goldston,** a brother I had the pleasure of meeting and growing up with more than thirty years ago, although 2, 200 miles have separated us for 26 years now, we have remained and will always be brothers! I would also be amiss if I did not acknowledge all of the great mentors, (**Spiritual advisors**), the *LORD* has placed in my life over the years. **Anointed men of *GOD*, like Pastors C. L. Smith of Love Sanctuary, Joe Hunt and Steve Miller of Epicenter, Jentzen Franklin and his associate Pastors Ben, Jabin and Jovan of Free Chapel Orange County, Bishop Ealy of Grace Memorial, Imam Ibrahim Pasha of Atlanta, may Allah be pleased with him, Imam Omar of Masjid Al-Shareef, Imam Yusuf Islam, may Allah be pleased with him and Imams Ron El-Amin** *and* **Kamal Abdul-Jabbar,** and so many others. *God bless you!* And, *I Thank You!*

DEDICATION

This book is dedicated to the Love and Mercy of **GOD Almighty,** and to the favor of **GOD,** one of many is allowing me to be the student of *Mrs. Rawls*, my High school English Literature Teacher, whose influence in this young and impressionable life left an indelible impact. I know you're smiling down upon me *Mrs. Rawls,* yet critically critiquing me to make sure that all of my punctuation and grammar is correct....(Smiling).

CHAPTER 1

"The Awakening"

6:45 A.M....December 15, 1995......I awakened with the reservations and portent sentiments of one wearily approaching this day! In spite of the gentle feminine ways my fiancé employed most mornings to arouse me, I deliberately laid there, motionless, as she appealed to me: ***"Ken baby, come now, get up sweetheart, we've got to get ready.*** I cannot deny though, the repetitive preparations and journeys over the past five months, (to and from court), kept me and all my relatives, friends, and close associates on an emotional rollercoaster! It was under this duress that I yearned to get this over with! No matter how challenging the experiences that lie ahead might be, I needed to breathe a sigh of relief, even if it be temporary!

My last three visits to Superior Court were very tense mornings! According to my attorney, I could have been remanded to custody on any of those appearances. Yet for one reason or another, my case got reset, (nothing to do with my humble petition, ***Cruise waiver,*** time to get legitimate life issues in order before sentencing). The varying impressions drawn from the Judge's decisions to keep resetting my court dates seemed to have a tint of mercy. It became apparent to me early on that my love ones drew from this what they hoped for.

My sons, with their youthful vigor and innocence, (15 and 17 at that time), would always say: "See Dad, you are not going anywhere maaannn!" Then both of them would grab me from each side with the most genuine embraces! I worried about them the most! Although arrangements have been made for them to live with their big uncle, my youngest brother Tony, after I'm gone, I just couldn't leave them yet, they just weren't ready to accept the truth. My Lion cubs will have to transition into manhood without my physical presence. In spite of my extensive conversations with them about the desperate, irresponsible act I committed, and the very serious consequences I must now face because of it, they refused to accept the inevitable...

My brother Tony and me in Moreno Valley, CA. /1993

My brother Tony would utter a real sigh of relief when contacted, realizing I was on the streets a couple weeks more, and insisted emphatically that I meet him after work to share another powerful fraternal experience, as always! My mother and all my siblings back home in Atlanta sent their heartfelt messages of love and support, encouraging me to keep the faith. Our close friends, (Terry, Nancy, Donald, John, Eric, Don, Robert and others), expressed their elation that I was granted more time to share, hope, pray, along with them for a merciful disposition, or perhaps some miraculous course of events that might cause the court to probate my sentence instead.

Terri and I always viewed those reschedules as another favor from **GOD**! As soon as the hearing was over, we would embrace all the way back to the car, dancing and rejoicing in the power of love as we tastefully taunted and teased each other with titillating descriptions of the passionate rapture that awaited us as soon as we got home! For now, she, like I, could escape the fear and uncertainty that surrounded us. For Terri, my queen, my love, my soulmate, was also my co-defendant! This would prove to be one of my painful regrets! That I would allow my lady to be involved in that harrowing act, even remotely.

"Hindsight can only be of real benefit to any of us, when the wisdom gained is applied in future experiences, and discretion is and shall forever be the better part of valor!"

On this December morning, as I moved drudgingly about, a battery of thoughts and visions circulated inside my head at race car speed! I thought initially of how time really does fly! Why it seemed as if just a week ago I was in suit and tie, sitting in Superior court, weighing the possibilities! Before my last two court appearances my attorney did reiterate that I could be remanded to custody during any of those hearings, and before this one, **"Bring your toothbrush!"**

So today is the day that the uncertainty ends, and new, unfamiliar journeys will begin? As Terri and I passed each other in our cozy, one bedroom apartment, I thought about my last court appearance with her. This morning we chose to look at each other through peripheral parameters only, knowing and understanding that one moment's stare in each other's eyes would be potentially volatile, capable of unleashing flood gates of tears and regrets on this fateful morning, and would only serve to delay us even more.

In Terri's case, because of her minimal, consequential involvement, we were sure she would be a candidate for probation. Her attorney employed the strategy of keeping our cases separate in court. There were two other co-defendants, one that had already **"sang like a canary"**, and cut a deal with the D.A.'s office, and the other one, **"a fugitive at large!"** Terri and I had been out of jail since June, and in light of this fact, the D.A.'s office was growing impatient and zealously sought a conviction in this case. It was due to the advice of Terri's attorney, in conjunction with the D.A.'s office that kept insisting that if a **"ring leader," a protagonist"** could be sentenced before Terri's case began its final stages of deliberation, she could receive even more leniency. Well, *I am that "protagonist!"*

> "The hungry Judges soon the sentence sign, and
> wretches hang that Jurymen may dine."
>
> ALEXANDER POPE

But, as some precarious circumstance would have it, statements from a co-defendant in this case limited the options available to Terri, and upon the advice of her attorney she accepted a plea bargain for two years with half-time considerations. So there I stood, frozen in my steps, as my mind's eye attempted to focus on a visualization. ***"Fog filled pictures have these intrinsic thoughts painted!"***

What would the court setting be like today? How would the Judge rule in my case? According to my attorney, I could receive between eight and nineteen years...

"Litigant: A person about to give up his skin
for the hope of retaining his bone!"

AMBROSE BIERCE

I had been offered plea bargains twice before in my case, I refused them. **Timing is essential in everything.** At the times these plea bargains were offered, my life was in a dismal state, incongruent with me and all those I loved and cared for! *I couldn't go yet!* My sons were residing with my brother Tony. Terri and I were residing with close friends, and all our furniture and other personal effects were in storage. The security and stability we had known as a family eluded us! I wanted to, I needed to make amends with all those my reckless conduct had injured! Over the weeks since our initial court appearances, Terri and I worked diligently to secure another apartment, another automobile, employment, and all the other tangibles that would ensure the re-establishment and exchange of the wonderful sense of family we had all grown to know. In spite of the pending outcome these court appearances represented, (separation due to incarceration), we would spend whatever time we had left together as lovingly and constructively as possible, *ideally.*

> "In war, as in life, it is often necessary, when some cherished scheme has failed, to take up the best alternative open, and if so, it is folly not to work at it with all your might."
>
> WINSTON CHURCHILL

In the midst of these pursuits, I often wondered how Terri would react when the Judge sealed my fate with the force of her gavel, and the Bailiff or Deputy Sheriff pulled me away from the comfort and security of her embrace. Or, how would I react for that matter, knowing I had, at this point, relinquished all my rights and liberties to others? That even the facile discretion to touch her face, to kiss her; to wrestle with my sons, to humor and laugh with my only daughter, (Ms. Kenya); to debate the issues of the day with my brothers; basic correspondence with all my love ones back home; to embrace them all as only I could do, **was not mine anymore! This basic human discretion was not mine anymore!**

> "Liberty means responsibility, this is why many men dread it."
>
> GEORGE BERNARD SHAW

Daddy, (a pet name Terri called me), resounded in my left ear, yet my thoughts kept me captive inside this daydream. She called me again, Daddy! Huh, huh? I replied. Here's a cup of coffee, your clothes are pressed and ready, and I prepared you a breakfast sandwich, it's on the table. I said thank you, and then she kissed me oh so gently on the lips. While getting dressed, I remember the insensate experience of not remembering putting on my socks, or buttoning my shirt. I remember standing in front of the mirror putting on my neck tie, and looking at myself in the mirror and seeing no reflection, just clothes, a long sleeve shirt with no hands protruding, a collar with no neck or head protruding, just animated clothing, moving about with the agility and purpose of human flesh! I sat down on the side of the bed while sipping my coffee. My mind took flight on me again...I saw vivid imagery of the colorful family dinner and the formal proposal made in the presence of everyone, nearly a year ago, **when I asked Terri to marry me.**

What a perfect setting it was too! **December 25, 1994...** Our home was warm and quite accommodating. Terri's mother, Aunt, and cousins traveled from other parts of the country to be with us during this holiday season. My brother Tony and his family joined us for dinner, only my brother and my sons knew the very special request I planned to make of Terri on this day. The glow, warmth and crackling of the fireplace , the aroma of smoked turkey, prime rib, collard greens and baking dressing, the colors and decorations, the fresh pine smell of a twelve foot evergreen tree under which lie colorful stacks of neatly wrapped gifts.

The beautiful floral arrangements and the symphony of conversations and laughter created the perfect type of ambience most appropriate for the kind of heartfelt expressions of love I planned to declare to Terri as I asked her to take my hand in marriage. I asked for everyone's undivided attention as I lit two red candles sticking out of the holiday bouquet I had given Terri. I dimmed the lighting and asked that everyone join me around the dining room table and I asked Terri to please take a seat in the chair I pulled out for her. I kneeled down on my right knee and recited this poem I compiled exclusively for this occasion....

"Will You Marry Me"
There was a strong desire within my heart,
To a find a companion to have an intricate part.
In a very serious venture, a vision from above,
Laced with thoughts of paradise, filled with love.
So with you my love I promise to do my best,
For with you sweetheart, I've fulfilled my quest!
Wherever you are is where I always long to be,
Terri, the love of my life, "Will You Marry Me?"
KBA

I placed my hand behind my back as previously rehearsed, my son Mikal placed the black velvet case in my hand that contained the three quarter carat diamond engagement ring. I opened the case, took the ring out and placed it on the ring finger of Terri's left hand. The room was overwhelmed with ooooooooooooo's and aaaaaahhhhhh's!! Tears began to roll down Terri's cheeks, her mother's cheeks, her Aunt's cheeks, and before long, all the women were crying tears of joy and elation! Terri was so overwhelmed with emotion that she forgot to answer my proposal. Her mother said "Teddy", (a nickname for her only child), what is your answer? Terri smiled and replied: yes, yes, yes! She turned to face me, took me in her arms and kissed me intensely while cameras flashed and love ones applauded. Everyone seemed to radiate love and happiness. Terri's mother embraced me and called me son, as everyone sat down to enjoy the ceremonial feast!

> "For each ecstatic instant we must anguish pay,
> in keen and quivering ratio to the ecstasy."
>
> EMILY DICKERSON

The familiar prances of Inu kitty, (our family pet), as she brushed her body against my back, jarred me out of the trance like daze of reminiscence I had drifted into. I checked my watch, it was now **7:17 A.M.**....I left the bedroom and joined Terri at the dining room table. There I attempted to consume the cold yet colorful breakfast sandwich she had prepared for me. There, in our dining room, where we enjoyed many delectable meals together, there, at that table, our awkwardly implicit behavior towards each other said it all! **Yes, this is the day!**

   I compiled a final checklist to ensure that all I needed done had been addressed, or would be…

   (1). The boys, **(Mikal and Hakim)**, are *safe and secure*. **They are secure??** They are situated with my brother Tony. This is an arrangement we all understood would be in the best interest of the boys. I am eternally grateful that **GOD** blessed me to spend the valuable time and colorful experiences that we have been blessed to spend together, yes, we are very close. When people saw us together, they thought we were brothers. They matured into such fine young men.

I knew this dilemma before me was especially dolorous for them! I had done all that I could, and more, over the past several months, to prepare them for my inevitable departure. I explained to them, ***the error of my ways!*** I cried with them, consoled them, I comforted them and encouraged them. I even made a ***pact*** with them. I called their attention to the challenges that lie ahead, that this is our time to shine apart. For so long the light of our love and loyalty had safeguarded each other, ***yet now, it was time to test the strength of their wings and training.*** I proffered them, their ***Rights of Passage...***

"MIKAL and HAKIM" The Rights of Passage"
The rights of passage were very strong traditions practiced in Africa, the Motherland,
Where the elder men took the teenage boys to help them transition from a boy to a man.
They practiced how to hunt in the wild for hours, with great skill and very little motion,
They went to fish at the great lakes, torrent rivers, and made their way to the ocean.
They learned how to use every part of their catch, for food, clothing and even tools,
In the forests they cut down trees and learned to build houses, tables and even stools.
In the evening the boys and men would gather to talk about the woman and child,
The art of romance, roles and responsibilities, this discussion would last for a while.
Then at the evening meal they would talk about family and community as a whole,

How each and every child, woman and man in the village, plays a very important role.
Now for months they rehearsed their knowledge and skills, and all of them understood,
The responsibility they have to themselves, their families, and all their neighborhoods.
Though we're not in Africa, Black men have continued this, somehow, some way,
My sons **Mikal and Hakim, the rights of passage**, I must pass on to both of you today.
(1). First and foremost, you must pray, trust and acknowledge *GOD'S* divine grace,
(2). Learn ***HIS Revealed Word***, study and obey it, **HE** will guide you to that special place.
(3). Work hard to maintain good morals, precepts and priceless values in your life,
(4). Then **HE** will bless you with much prosperity, happiness, and little or no strife.
(5). Please stay away from the rumors, gossip, and small talk that people tend to say,
(6). When they ask why you don't hang out, say: **"I must follow the narrow way."**
(7). Never take anything into your bodies like alcohol, tobacco, and all man's drugs,
(8). Those things are so evil, just look at the good people that they turned into thugs!
(9). Develop the discipline to spend more time reading and writing, away from school,
(10). "I must work hard every day to enhance my own mind, should be your golden rule!"

(11) Above all, be loving, kind, and courteous to each other and all those that you meet,
(12). Remember: "The mark of a true warrior or winner is one who never accepts defeat!

KBA

Mikal and Hakim (Ages 17 and 15)

I promised my sons with sincerity of heart, that I would be a better person, (stronger and wiser), by the time I am released. Both of them gave me their word and pledge to work harder to be the best they could be. They agreed to look out for each other, and their mother and little sister too. *"I love my children very much!*

(2). I discussed with Terri the arrangement already made to forward my clothing and other personal effects to my brother Tony. Once her case approached closure she would have to begin the very tedious task of packing all our other stuff, much of it would be returned to storage. I acquired some new books, a colorful journal, and some other writing supplies I would need when I get situated on the "other side." Wherever they, **(*California Department of Corrections and Rehabilitation*),** decides to send me. I understand that could be anywhere in the State.

(3). I encouraged Terri to be sure to have our close friends, (Nancy, Donald, Robert, and Tracy), to accompany her to the courts for the remainder of her hearings. Her attorney assured us he could get her sentencing hearing postponed for several weeks. I knew she would need the moral support from all of them at those hearings because I would already be **"*remanded to custody.*"**

(4). I raked my brain for any final advice or instructions. I pondered all the statements and sentiments of love and penitence, I shared with Terri, my sons, Tony, and all of my love ones over the previous months. Had I said all that needed to be said? ***Probably not?*** I told Terri again how much I loved her, and how much I needed her in my life. I told her she must be strong in my absence, and assured her we would be together again when this is over. We caressed each other for a while, kissed, then we wiped away each other's tears.

> "While grief is fresh, every attempt
> to divert it only irritates."
>
> SAMUEL JOHNSON

> "Though He brings grief, He will show
> compassion, so great is His unfailing love."
>
> LAMENTATIONS 3:32

7:33 A. M.......As Terri and I prepared to leave our apartment, I took Inu kitty in my arms. I rubbed my hands slowly through her soft fur, the way she liked me to. As she purred, lying limp in my arms, I told her to be good, to take care of herself while I was away, and I would be back. We took the usual route to court, a fifteen minute drive straight down Magnolia Street. As we drove along, I recall perambulating everything in passing. Street signs; landmark buildings, shopping centers; Blockbuster Video; (a place we frequented); the Indigo Bookstore and Apparel Mart. All the adjacent neighborhoods I had come to know, and the wood streets that cross Magnolia.

Every few minutes I would fix my eyes on Terri's visage, ***carefully detailing every contour and feature.*** I ran my fore finger gently around her right ear, across her temple and down the side of her face, and under her chin then around her neck. I thought about all that we had been through, endured, and in some cases overcome. I thought about all the wonderful, color coordinated meals, all the sacrifices we had made for each other, for family. The calm and gentle approach Terri always took with the boys, at home and at school.

The way she washed, dried, and folded our clothes, carefully organizing and separating garments and fabrics accordingly, was uniquely her! All the hot baths and showers she and I shared together, scrubbing each other's hard to reach places with fragrant soaps and hand held porous scrubbers Terri purchased for us. All the eagerly anticipated massages and rub downs with pure cocoa butter or shea butter lotions that awaited us in the privacy of our bedroom. And man, oh man! The way this woman inveigled, titillated, and seduced me was truly unprecedented! Even our bodies seemed to be aerodynamically designed to fit each other! A perfect fit! I seized her with the fiery, insatiable desire of a hungry lion, every opportunity I got!

"Heart's Desire

For you Terri only, my heart is really falling, despite my own reason constantly calling.
Reminding me of the hurt I sustained in the past, when I allowed my heart to fall too, too fast.
To love you Terri is my own ever-present drive, but another heartache I may not survive.
I have arrived at a serious stage within my life, to find a real companion and not just a wife.
To terminate this search for true happiness, filled with mutual contentment and nothing less.
So until this dream is acquired I just won't tire, this is the real essence of my own **"Heart's Desire."**

KBA

"At the end of what is called the *"sexual life",* the only love which has lasted is the love which has everything, every disappointment, every failure, and every betrayal, which has accepted even the sad fact that in the end there is no desire as the simple desire for companionship."

Graham Greene

"For everything in the world-the lust of the flesh, the lust of the eyes, and the pride of life, comes not from the Father, but from the world."

1 JOHN 2: 16

CHAPTER 2

"ATTRTITION"

*By no means was our relationship without flaw
or its own share of difficulties. I do concur that
one of the most challenging experiences in all of
nature is the merging of two distinctively different
personalities and mentalities into a sense of oneness.*

*"Even the wisest of men make fools of
themselves about women, and even the most
foolish of women are wise about men."*

THEODOR REIK

WHEN YOU CONSIDER the idiosyncrasies diversely unique to African Americans, compounded by all of the contrasting definitions and ideologies this society offers for the very same terms and ideas, this merger becomes even more indurate. Terri and I were both confidently stubborn and we brought egos with us from worlds preceding this relationship. We both sought shelter with each other from the plastic, depraved dens of bit ballers and player players where most women are dehumanized as beautiful bundles of flesh and pleasure, *sex objects only,* and the men cater to this through the sharing of material resources and/or the promotion of drugs, lies and promiscuity, *a debauched, devalued life!*

> "Along with the idea of romantic love, she was introduced to another, ***physical beauty.*** Probably one of the most destructive ideas in the history of human thought. Both originated in envy, thrived in insecurity, and ended in delusion. In equating physical beauty with virtue, she stripped her mind, bound it, and collected self-contempt by the heap. She forgot lust and simple caring for. She regarded love as possessive mating, and romance as the goal of the spirit. It would be for her a well-spring from which she would draw some of the most destructive emotions, deceiving the lover and seeking to imprison the beloved, curtailing true freedom in every way."
>
> TONI MORRISON

I had, (overtime), hop-scotched my way through several caring relationships before, and since arriving in California. The very first relationship I developed here in California was with Willetta Whittenburg, a very loving and head strong independent Black woman that had her own business, and was instrumental in me being able to send for my boys a few months after I arrived in California. Interestingly enough, the catalyst that propelled me to California was in fact the separation from my wife, (my High school sweetheart). I was raised in an era when boys were trained and disciplined to be men early on! I was very fortunate to have strong male role models in my life from inception to departure that left an indelible impact on my life forever! So with that, I got married at age twenty. My ex-wife was seventeen. When things spiraled out of control with this relationship some seventeen years later, (with my young children and their mother and I now apart), after many years on the open seas, with many wonderful, scenic experiences over time to cherish, having endured many storms together, the unexpected happened, we ran ashore, *shipwrecked*!

"Re-Lation-Ship"

My experiences were few, yet I did love this girl, she came into my life and helped transform my world.
Before long she had my heart, so I cut the chase, by her side I just knew should be my special place.
So we agreed to navigate our futures together as one, we shared everything, so much loving fun.
Along came major difficulties that weren't in our favor, during this life storm, I couldn't save her.
So goes another relationship, sunken by our own ways, another sad statistic, these words display.
KBA

There are always those standing in the shadows, the spectators of life, whispering from the security of veiled darkness: I told you so; you got married too young; you were incompatible with one another anyway; I knew it wouldn't last. Annette and I met when she was thirteen, (a mature thirteen). I was sixteen. I will always remember that afternoon in High school, on the third floor hallway, in between classes.

That day my homeboy Steve and I saw her from a distance as she walked away. Her sculptured physique caught our attention, and on this day we made an arrogant bet, I'm going to make her my girl Steve, Nope, I'm going to make her my girl my homeboy retorted! I'll have her hand before school is out today, nope, not before me! Bet! Bet! I made it a matter of strategy to introduce myself to Annette at the earliest opportunity. She was so shy and timid!

We had to communicate through her girlfriend because she was too afraid to speak to me alone. Eventually I visited her home, met her family, and shared mutually constructive activities, (movies, picnics, and extra-curricular events after school), with Annette. A virgin, unsullied by the wilds of any man's perverted sexual fantasies. Her uninhibited feminine hormones, which found egress in the pores of her skin, a natural, fresh smell like that of newborn babies, aroused me whenever we were near.

After months of dialogue, sharing, and an increased fondness for each other, we did it! First in the backseat of my 1968 Ford Fairlane 500, and after that, as often as possible in the bedroom. Annette had her own bedroom, it was between her sister Daisy's bedroom and the main hallway of the house, and her mother's bedroom was directly across this hallway. Daisy's bedroom had a backdoor that opened to a spacious backyard. I learned to make use of this backdoor often! I would say goodnight to her mother, stepfather and grandmother, then wink at Daisy on my way out as a signal of my intended return.

I would hang out in the neighborhood for a couple of hours or return home until Annette called to say her mother was asleep. Then

I would park a couple of blocks away and under the veil of darkness I would maneuver through neighbors' backyards with the approach and agility of a seasoned spy, usually with a box of Church's fried chicken, sodas and candy bars for Daisy, (a small token of my appreciation for her cooperation and silence). I soon learned three very important lessons from this experience:

(1). Keep your adolescent daughters bedrooms away from exterior doors,

(2). Never underestimate the wit and cunning of a mother, especially one that suspects you may be sneaking across the back fence after hours, (a wood post fence at that!), and,

(3). *That really is how babies are made!*

After a few months I became negligent and complacent, climbing back and forth over that fence, even on a few occasions when I could see Annette's mother, (Eula Mae's), silhouette visible on the other side of the house. Early one Sunday morning, around five in the morning, I made my usual, weary climb over that fence. As I catapult myself up by grapping a wood post, I felt one sting, then another, then another, then many at once! In a matter of seconds I was running down those dark lifeless streets of that neighborhood, stripping off garments and kicking off my shoes as I oooweeeeddd and ooouuuccchhheddd in an unrestrained frenzy!

A whole nest of vicious hornets was on me, chasing me relentlessly as I screamed throughout those back streets! By the time I gathered my senses and recalled where my car was parked, I looked like a mob had stoned me with tiny pebbles, and I was down to my socks and underwear! I was so languished and embarrassed by this whole ordeal, I didn't bother to retrieve my shoes and clothing, I drove as I was!

I was so beat up by that experience that I stayed home for a few days. I informed Annette of what happened to me that morning, and I asked if she would please look to see if she could find my shoes and clothing and I would get them later. Though her mother never acknowledged that she set me up, long after that incident and even to this day, I believe she poured some honey or something on those wood posts to get me! **Mother and Nature got me!** A few months after this incident, **Annette missed her period.** She did the right thing and told her mother. After intense tribal inquests from both clans, it was decided that we were too young to be with child.

So Annette was required to abort the child. We got through the emotional fallout behind it, and after three years of dating, Annette and I were wed. The same year, our oldest son, (Mikal), was born. Twenty two months later, our second son, (Hakim), was born, and, ten years later our only daughter, (Kenya), was born. We grew up together, worshipped together, studied together and played together. Usually, if you saw me, you saw Annette. We started out on the right foot, the tragedy is that somewhere along the way in our trek upward, we lost cadence and got out of step with each other. I have no reason to be remorseful, Annette and I shared many wonderful years together, and together we have three beautiful children. ***I will always love her!***

> "No love, no friendship can cross the path of our destiny without leaving some mark on us forever."
>
> FRANCOIS MAURIAC

"DEPARTURE"

I wanted so badly for this experience to last, to be
true, I made so many sacrifices for the love of you.
We were so young and unfamiliar in this type of love,
yet unyielding to all obstacles, guided from above.
Myriad visions of beauty radiating from my heart,
about the family, us and paradise from the start.
We could have reached levels new, unreached yet,
the thought of this failure can't lead to regrets.
Lady, I tried to share every aspect of me, some things
you know of, others you will now never see.
Now our hearts are divided, in total contrast; under this continual duress you and I just won't last.
So it seems more vivid than ever, I must go; if this creative isn't clear to you, one day you will know.

KBA

So that player-player, big baller attitude was a tough outer skin that protected a very sensitive under layer. I refused to let my feelings exceed a certain point until I met Terri. Terri and I met at the shopping plaza where I was employed. She worked and lived in close proximity to the plaza, so over the course of several months we would see each other frequently, pausing to dialogue about this or that. One evening Terri came to the plaza on her bicycle. She did some unexpected shopping and couldn't transport her purchases home on the bike so she asked if I would bring them by after work and the rest is history! In hindsight I believe it was all planned. (Smile). She proved to be the hostess with the mostess! A smile so congenial and warm, a real earth shaker, and a masterfully sculpted body, like Josephine Baker! Terri had the skillful, unmatchable ability to capture a man's heart if she chose to, she knew how to get what she wanted from a man!

> "She was not likely to be the kind of woman to settle for equality when sex gave her the advantage."
>
> ANTHONY DELANO

I felt Terri had met her equal or even superior in me though! A Renaissance man is what I have sought to be for years. I operated with the smooth conversation and ardently amiable demeanor; debonair, and impenetrable certitude of a man well read and seasoned well in culture and experience. I was bold, daring and conscientiously grounded! I entertained Terri and romanced her with poetry, flowers, and tangible dreams and hopes of what we could achieve together, and I had an insatiable appetite her for love and affection!

> "I have met with women who I really think would like to be married to a poem and to be given away by a novel."
>
> JOHN KEATS

"A BEAUTIFUL LADY"

Please pardon me if it appears that I stare, but you
look so amazingly gorgeous, standing there!
Like the finest of jewels, a rare and very precious
stone, in a very large crowd you do stand alone!

The contour of your succulent lips, compliments
your smile, and the way you walk exudes style!
Like Queen Nefertiti, the depth of those eyes, can
leave the strongest of men quite hypnotized!
You possess many features that are rare and unique,
just one of many is your vivacious physique!
So please take my hand and come take a walk with me, for
you're the finest of women, **"A BEAUTIFUL LADY!"**
KBA

"We are not deceived, we deceive ourselves."

GOETHE

Within three months of our initial date, Terri was pregnant and passionately pleading with me to move in with her! Though I had fallen head over heels for Terri, I wasn't sure what to do with these rapidly developing feelings and circumstances. Besides, there was Elizabeth. A copper-toned, cat-eyed Islander from the Virgin Isles. I met her in Moreno Valley while heading to the gym, (I was driving and she was power walking down the street). She was so beautiful! I had to stop the car and go power walking behind her! That was more than a year before meeting Terri, and we now lived together. Elizabeth, her sister, her two kids, my sons and I shared a home together. Elizabeth and I had grown a bit distant in our relationship prior to me meeting Terri, and I was honest with Terri, telling her initially that I was involved with and lived with another woman, and soon, Elizabeth would know about Terri. Over the next few weeks I was like a caged lion!

Terri was quite adamant about having the baby. I wasn't as excited as she was about the baby, yet I respected the woman's right to choose. My relationship with Elizabeth grew and matured quite rapidly. I can't deny though, I did care about Elizabeth and did not want to see her hurt. I know she really cared about me and my sons too. Elizabeth was a beautiful Virgin Islander with a reserved, genteel presence. She felt so fragile in my arms, yet she was strong and athletic, jogging and aerobicizing regularly. I felt a strong sense of responsibility toward Elizabeth and the children, yet I was unhappy and uncertain about our future together. On one hand there was Terri, our recent conception and the obvious compatibility that permeated everything that we shared. I felt so at ease and peaceful around her. I found myself longing for her more and more. On the other hand, there was Elizabeth, I cared for her, and she held a special place in my heart.

The thought of leaving her was unpleasant to say the least. We had our moments, during which Elizabeth shared some of the pain and heartache associated with past relationships. This proved to be a very trying time! I lost sleep, weight, and my appetite, running from one side of town to the other. I had to do something, my time, energy, and heart were literally **torn apart**!

"TORN"
Wedged between to loving affairs, pondering over others' dos and dares.
I never imaged things happening this way,
now I can't find proper words to say.
One love falters, another is born, and I care
for both people, now I'm torn!

> I know a decision is what I must make, the
> best decision for love's sake.
> Being in this situation I do scorn, some-
> thing must give, I can't last long
> **"TORN!"**
> KBA

> "The happiness of a man in this life does not consist
> in the absence but in the mastery of his passions."
>
> ALFRED, LORD TENNYSON

Elizabeth, with her sensitive nature and intuitive mind, began to detect the unsettling condition this situation placed me in. The languor I exhibited around the house and in the bedroom must have been terrifyingly familiar, and instead of posing any questions about this state, she started to examine my activities much closer, even conducting her own surveillance as she followed me from time to time. One evening after leaving Terri's apartment complex, I recognized Elizabeth's car in my rearview mirror. As I sped up, she did too! No evasive driving maneuvers seemed to work, she managed to stay within three car lengths of me. She chased me all the way home to Moreno Valley! I arrived first, I jumped out the car, went in the house, greeted the children and went directly to the bedroom, anticipating the bombardment of an emotionally charged inquest! Within ten minutes Elizabeth entered the house and came directly to the bedroom, slamming the door behind her!

  The expression on her face exuded an air of confidence toward the issue at hand. She sat down on the bed across from me and began to cry! She uttered these words amidst her sobs: How could you do this to me? All I could say was I am so sorry, I never intended to hurt you! Elizabeth began divulging all the information she had acquired about Terri. She knew her address, her place of employment, how long she had been employed there, her age, she even knew her phone number. She demanded to know what Terri meant to me, how long I've known her, and if I loved her.

I expounded as delicately as I could about what I think happened with us, about my present relations with Terri, I even told her about the pregnancy. Elizabeth cried and cried! I did everything I could to console her, I never intended to hurt her like this. Nothing could have prepared me for the unexpected resolve Elizabeth would take after my declaration of unfaithfulness! Elizabeth turned to be with the light of love and loyalty in her eyes and said: *What are you going to do baby?*

Do you love her? I love you man, and we can overcome this trial together, if you still want me! Dam! My heart jumped from my chest to my throat! The dismay her statement created left me more bewildered than ever!

> "What dire offence from amorous causes spring,
> what mighty contests rise from trivial things."
>
> ALEXANDER POPE

Her words reverberated in my head like an echo chamber! I knew I really cared for Elizabeth. I loved and admired her gentle feminine ways. But now my own trepidation overshadowed all of that! I had hurt her severely! I wanted to believe her, yet I was afraid of any retribution she might decide to exact towards me at a later date! I have seen numerous incidents over the years, where scorned lovers or vengeful women struck back at their counterparts and it wasn't a pretty site! A very personal experience involved one of my older brothers, he was shot in the neck with his own gun by a live-in lover and barely escaped death! Another one involved my homeboy Virgil; a player by the time he was fifteen, dating older women that took care of him financially. One of them found out about his infidelity and stabbed him in his heart while he slept! I believe in that old adage: **"Hell knows no fury like that of a woman scorned!"**

    I stayed with Elizabeth that night. My gestures of consolation and compassion eventually led to hot, passionate sex! I assured her that I would work this controversy out. I was not sure what I wanted to do or what was best. I didn't sleep much that night, and very little in the early morning hours as I pensively ruminated over the pros and cons of this present dilemma. The following day I visited Terri at work before going to work myself, I wasn't sure of the words my confused heart intended to say as the elevator opened to the fifth floor lobby. The very first site that my weary eyes focused on was Terri and Elizabeth seated across from each other in the lobby.

    I was determined not to let the emotions raging through me seem apparent to either one of them. I greeted them both, Terri, Elizabeth… Then Elizabeth replied sardonically: Here is the man all of this discussion is about. I looked at Elizabeth, then at Terri, then back at Elizabeth. Terri said absolutely nothing, then she got up and walked back toward her office door while staring at me with a look that was so piercing that I felt her eyes cutting through me like that of a Swiss blade! Elizabeth and I boarded the elevator together down to the ground floor.

While alone on the elevator I asked Elizabeth what she hoped to gain by doing this. What did she say to Terri? Elizabeth replied emphatically: I told her to stay away from my man, or else! I asked her: or else what? And she retorted: I won't be nice the next time I see her! I was furious and astonished at the same time! Angry that Elizabeth had resorted to such drastic measures, yet awed at her bold, brash approach. I explained to Elizabeth that she should not direct any hostilities and/or anxieties towards Terri, I was the blame for all of this! And on that note, I embraced her and walked across the street to work. I phoned Terri immediately and apologized for the embarrassment I knew that confrontation had caused her at work. She was acerbic towards me as she blamed me for the ignominy Elizabeth's presence and demeanor created at her job.

After several minutes of humble discourse, I convinced Terri to meet me at the Carlos O' Brien's restaurant and bar that we frequented. I stood in the parking lot of the plaza awaiting Terri's arrival. Her office was in walking distance and most days she chose to walk to the plaza. I identified with her unique statuesque physique from a distance, that colorful image of her graceful, yet athletic strides as she approached, my heart reverberated in my throat! Then that voice within that speaks clear and profoundly at times like this; who are you fooling? \Not me, you really do love this woman! Terri refused the offer my patulous arms suggested. I pulled open the door to the restaurant as she swung through with poise and style, not failing to sneer at me in passing. We sat across from each other at our usual table, in a cozy corner away from the lunch crowd.

I knew all of the staff there, so we were treated with the warmth and genuineness of family. The tension at our table must have been like a fog! A familiar waitress brought over chips and salsa, and sodas, then left us alone for the rest of our stay. I could tell Terri was deliberately avoiding looking me in my eyes, trying hard to get a handle on her composure. Before she completed her first statement, her eyes glazed over, and a tear rolled rapidly down her left cheek. I took a napkin from our table and handed it to her as tears began to flow randomly! I tried sincerely to calm her, she raised her head and said with uneasiness and congestion in her voice: I can't do this anymore, I'm sorry, I do love you baby, but this is too much!

We've been seeing each other for four months now, and on top of that, I'm carrying your baby, and you can't decide if you want to be with me or not! Then, on top of all this, this woman, Elizabeth, She's stalking me! How did she find out about my job? What else does she know about me Ken? This is it! I must say goodbye! As she got up from our table, I asked her to please give me an opportunity to share my recent revelations too, about her and the baby. She declined my offer, got up and walked out of the restaurant without looking back!

"When we quarrel, how we wish we were blameless."

RALPH WALDO EMERSON

The last hour with Terri reverberated in my mind, and caused me to rethink what I had gone through over the past four months. Over the next few weeks I didn't even call Terri. In my insecure world of foolish pride and egotism, ***I'm the man! That's right, I'm the man!***

> "Pride is seldom delicate, it will please
> itself with very mean advantages."
>
> SAMUEL JOHNSON

I did all I could to stop ruminating about her, the baby, and me. I even tried to divert attention and energy from this and placed it in my workouts and training. I would jog until I nearly passed out from exhaustion and dehydration, or I would workout with the weights until my muscles lost all flexibility and I was stiff as a board! I tried to block her out of mind by thinking only of Elizabeth and the children. I put more zest in my relationship with Elizabeth, and spent more time at home with the children, playing games, studying and checking homework assignments.

Yet all I saw, smelled and craved, was Terri! I missed her infectious laughter, her gentle, yet firm touch, and even her cooking made everything I ate at home seem bland, like cardboard! An internal query haunted me, it asked me constantly: **What has this woman done to you?** Some old folklore entered my head about **roots** and **moe joes** humorously. I never believed in those superstitions. I thought about the sex, was I whipped? No, it was so much more than any temporal feeling or experience. This along with the tightened, distrusting reign Elizabeth began to exercise to protect what she perceived to be her's, **Me,** was just too much!

> "Things forbidden have a hidden charm."
>
> SENECA

If I went to the basketball court; the corner market; to hang out with my brother Tony, she wanted to go. If I said no, she would look at me askance, understandably so, I had violated our trust. If I invited her to go along she would hang on to me like static cling. After a few weeks of uncompromising discipline, and internal turmoil, I rescinded my previous stance. I had to call her, and now I was ready to tell Terri just how much I needed her and loved her, ***I'd rather me with you!***

I"D RATHER BE WITH YOU!"
Out of all the activities I prefer to do, I'm convinced now my love, "I'd rather be with you!"
Clear visions of you throughout my dreams, consistently flowing just like natures streams.
Now I've held you close, captured in your arms, while subjected to your beauty and charms.
The way you touched me in your own special way, left memories with me that are here to stay!
No more doubts prevail lady, your love is true, and so I called to say: **"I'D RATHER BE WITH YOU!"**
KBA

I called Terri the following day at work, the excitement and enthusiasm in her voice suggested she had really missed me, she asked why I hadn't called her. I told her we needed to meet as soon possible and I would explain everything then. We agreed to see each other later that evening. I told my sons about Terri, and the dilemma I had created with Elizabeth. I had them accompany me to meet Terri for the very first time. We arrived around seven o clock, I had the boys stand to the side of the door while I knocked, and Terri didn't know I brought them with me. Terri answered the door with her usual charm and warm smile I had grown so fond of. I entered the apartment, embraced and kissed Terri, and before she could say a word, I said: There's someone else with me that would like to see you.

I went to the door and gestured for the boys to come in. They introduced themselves, and the ardent embraces and genuine smiles and laughter said that it was love at first sight between these three! Well, for the rest of the evening, it was as if I wasn't even there! The comfort and ease they displayed around each other was similar to old friends reunited after a long period of time. For the next three weeks, it was Terri and the boys, they were inseparable! Every time I looked up, they were going somewhere, the San Diego Zoo; to a youth conference in Los Angeles; to the shopping malls; to the movies, etc…

The boys grew fonder and fonder of Terri with each visit. The stage was now set! I sat down with Terri, conveyed my innermost thoughts and feelings about us, the boys, and the baby. I asked her to please be for me, because: **"I'M FOR YOU!"**

"I'M FOR YOU!"

In the beginning I did have some reservations, though
I admired the sweet melody of your conversation.
Then we arranged to share some mutually positive
events, we both knew it was time that was well spent.
You do possess certain qualities that are special and
unique, creating an air of curiosity and mystique.
Then you touched me in your myriad colors and ways;
thoughts of you on my mind for days and days!

This is my heart speaking woman, I know it must be true, please be for me, because **"I'M FOR YOU!**
KBA

"The heart has its own reasons which
reason knows nothing of."

BLAISE PASCO"

Terri and I discussed the conditions of our merger, she shared some concerns about the pregnancy, whether it would be feasible to have a newborn right now. I gave my earnest views and support to her, I wanted the baby, yet I would allow her to make the choice, the final decision was her's to make. We agreed there was no reason for us to be apart any longer, which meant, there was only one thing left for me to do, leave Elizabeth. Elizabeth had mentioned to me that if I were to leave her, she would move back to her home, a place she hadn't been to in five years, the Virgin Isles.

After much painful discourse, I left Elizabeth, and the boys and I moved in with Terri. .Elizabeth and her two children moved back to the Islands. She called me at work once to let me know that the transition back home had been smooth, and if I was ever in the Virgin Islands, do look her up. That was the very last time I heard from her! It seems sort of ironic that the same day we moved with Terri, is the very same day she aborted our child. I will always remember these transitions, a merger of ***"attrition!"***

"ATTRITION"

Oh what a tangled web we inevitably weave, when
in practice with others we do deceive.

Whether it be malicious, or an inadvertent act,
the deeds we sow, one day will come back.
My reckless wanderings I cannot explain, have I
hurt others because of my own internal pain?
This is it! Be it a futile act or fruition! No more! I
have learned from this painful **"ATTRITION!"**
KBA

"The two most important dates in our lives are
when we are born and when we find out why."

MARK TWAIN

CHAPTER 3

"The Sentence"

7:50 A.M...........As Terri drove into the parking space adjacent to the courthouse and the car came to a stop, the overwhelming presence of the Richard Presley Hall of Justice building seemed to subdue me like never before. A trepidation seized my limbs, it was as if I was about to be swallowed up by some giant prehistoric creature! I sat in the car a few minutes and watched as all of the lawyers, jurors, victims, defendants and their family members formed several lines at the entrance of the building, preparing themselves to go through the metal detectors and security measures awaiting us at the front door. Terri and I kissed and embraced before leaving the car.

We walked hand and hand to the rear of the line, trying to display the kind of optimism we exchanged on previous court appearances, and this appearance would be like so many others wherein I was sent home once more for one reason or another. Terri turned to me and affirmed that she was hoping the exact same thing I was, by saying: Baby, don't be surprised if we are in and out of there in thirty minutes or less. I've got a feeling you're going back home with me! Then she leaned over and kissed me on my cheek and whispered sweet promises in my ear!

I smiled at her enthusiasm yet I made no reply. After going through the checkpoints, we examined the court calendar to make sure there had been no last minute shuffles in my assigned court room. We boarded the elevator to the fourth floor, clinching each other's hands tightly as the elevator ascended. The bell rang as the number four on the overhead panel lit up. The doors opened slowly, and Terri and I stepped out into the lobby. There stood the usual crowds of people surrounding each courtroom. Some of them were seated on the recessed benches, while others crowded the walls adjacent to the courtrooms, nervously awaiting the deputies' daily reading of the rules of the court, before anyone would be granted access.

Terri and I found a place for two on one of the benches. It was there amidst the noise and activity, that my mind took flight with me again. I gazed at Terri and pondered all that we had gone through, all of the factors that contributed to Terri and I committing that desperate act. She and I lost the security of good jobs a few weeks apart. We both had the love and respect of friends and neighbors alike. Ideal citizens in the eyes of so many! In retrospect it's clearer to me than ever before, we lived too close to the edge, for the here and now, instead of being frugal, and leaving a cushion for those rainy days, **the difficult times.**

> "It is hard to free fools from the chains they revere."
>
> VOLTAIRE

I realize and accept without reservations now, a common erroneous belief that anyone can juggle both worlds, the worlds of good and bad, right and wrong, truth and falsehood, and at the same time remain unsullied through the process is one of the most damaging misconceptions in the history of human thought and existence.

> "Such a person is double minded and
> unstable in all they do."
>
> *JAMES 1:8*

> "Ill habits gather by unseen degrees, as
> brooks make rivers, rivers run to seas."
>
> *JOHN DRYDEN*

Consistency means everything when it comes to our lifestyles. The vices of drug use, alcohol, and tobacco were not designed to be used in socially polite settings only. The reality is the stronger the addiction capability, the stronger the capital potential is. Though Terri and I did most of our indulgences in vice at home, it did not diminish the adverse effect they would have on us in short order. My drugs of choice for years were alcohol, usually beer, and cannabis for years. I took my first drink of alcohol, (Ole Kentucky Bourbon), when I was seven; smoked my first marijuana joint when I was thirteen, and inhaled my first cigarette when I was nine. There is no innocence in vice and folly, they strip us of our shame and commit us, unknowingly first, but not for long, to do their dance, their sinful, nasty dance!

> "Be alert and of sober mind."
>
> *1 PETER 5:8*

These vices become crutches overnight and we turn to them, especially when challenged with great difficulties, like a sweaty runner reaches for water to quench his demanding thirst! Being creatures of habit, we turn to those things we practice, **good or bad.** We lost one of our love ones, a soldier that left a void which can never be filled by anyone else due to the uncontrollable urge to drink alcohol… We miss you folks! **Terry (Pee Wee) Willis…** (08/28/1967-01/24/2012).

Over the years, some of my siblings and I struggled with some form of addictive behavior, whether it be tobacco, alcohol or drugs. I remember my father speaking to this one day, saying we had better be careful because he felt that we may have an addictive predisposition. Years later I was no longer in denial, after recognizing this uncontrollable urge to drink myself into oblivion, no matter the event or circumstance, and as a result of this awakening I began to feel guilty and convicted, so I ran to the safe refuge and effective program of Alcoholics Anonymous…

> "Drunkenness is nothing but voluntary madness."
>
> SENECA

The deferred anxiety we subject others to during these emotional roller-coasters, crash landings is ugly to say the least. I thought about some of my own trespasses remorsefully, against friends and family too.

> "What benefit did you reap at that time from
> the things you are now ashamed of?"
>
> ROMANS 6:21

"Trouble will rain on those who already wet."

Anonymous

In the very same week that I lost my job; Terri's company downsized and began to juggle the remaining employees around; my mentor, my friend, my father, **Bacadee,** as he was commonly called by his children and other family members, without warning or impending illness, **died suddenly of a massive heart attack!** My brother Tony, his family, Terri, the boys and I jumped in a leased van and drove all the way across country to Atlanta in a little less than thirty six hours! My father and I had our differences and father/son challenges over the years, he told me it was because I was too much like him, ***I loved him even more for it!*** I spoke to him less than two days before his demise, he did sound like he was tired. I wasn't really prepared for this, ***I was devastated!***

"Let us eat and drink, for tomorrow we shall die"

Isiah 22:13

"BACADEE"

What standard should we use, when men of our history we determine to carefully evaluate?
What was it about them? Was it their words, views, or other qualities that made them great?
I have a personal, fervent story, a real time testament that has to rank amongst the very best!
A man of courage, valor; the epitome of personal sacrifice, love and loyalty, his own life quest!

Born in a time in this country, when people of color were disenfranchised and oppressed,
Born in the South to a very strong family, that demanded excellence and nothing less!
Raised with those old fashioned values, that certainly shaped him from a boy into a man.
Inducted into the Armed Forces during the Korean War, off he goes to fight for this land!
Upon completion of his tour overseas, he enrolled in school at the university, Morris Brown,
To enhance his knowledge and career choices, and to start a family, it's time to settle down.
Written in the stars was the name of his beautiful soulmate, his very own heart's desire.
GOD sealed the fates of him and his lovely soulmate, he fell in love with **Gloria Shropshire!**
From this life long, powerful union, four amazing girls and five strong boys were made,
And a dogma truly unprecedented in our family, community and city would be firmly laid!
This unselfish husband and father worked his butt off, two jobs sometimes even three!
To ensure that his wife and children's needs and most wants were always met, completely!
He held high, **GOD**, the **Church** and **good education** as the true pathways to liberation.
And he gave his very last dollar to see all of us succeed, without the slightest hesitation!

A community activist with the youth, as he strolled through
the different neighborhoods,
The drugs and addiction; decrepit storefronts; misguided
young people, he really understood.
That we must be our **Brother's Keeper**, and without
hard work, there can be no reversal!
That we all should strive as in a race for our lives! He would
say: **This is no dress rehearsal!**
So I declare to all of you that listened or read these words,
this man's life is clearly exemplary!
As we stand here in honor and loving memory, of this
great man, my father, **"BACADEE!"**
KBA

We remained in Atlanta several days after Bacadee's funeral. I did some needed repairs around the old homestead for my mother. The time I got to spend with family and old friends was priceless, and even seemed sort of strangely similar to a celebrated reunion of one about to embark on a long, far away journey, not knowing if or when I would see them all again. This was Terri's initial acquaintance with all my family, and with her normal charm and warmth, they all found her very congenial and loving. Even my daughter Kenya, wanted to be in her company every chance she got.

We spent our last evening in Atlanta at 365 Lincoln Street, the place we were all raised. We loaded the van, said our goodbyes, and conducted a prayer circle in the front yard. We accounted for everyone and everything, then drove into the darkness of that night, beginning our long trek back across this vast and colorful land. We were not as expeditious going back as we were leaving California. We even stopped off in Dallas to visit with Terri's mother and with Tony's wife, (Sonya's) mother. Dallas left an indelible impact on me forever! **On the lawn of the downtown square was a National Historic plaque and right behind it were chains my ancestors once wore, and the holding shed no bigger than an old outhouse where slaves were packed into waiting to be auctioned off on the wood platform adjacent to it!** I was sick to my stomach at the sight of it! We couldn't get out of Dallas fast enough for me! By the grace of **GOD** we made it across this country and back without one accident or incident along the way. We were all beaten down by the journey. There is no rest for the weary*!*

"Anxiety is the interest paid on trouble before it is due."

WILLIAM R. INGE

Terri and I returned to greater financial and emotional stress. We used the majority of our reserved resources to assist with that necessary trek across country. A few days after returning to California, one my close associates, (Doc), that I made substantial money with got busted. Within a month, outstanding accumulated debts began to mount. Creditors began their persistent calls day and night. We used our talents and abilities to think of resourceful ways to make ends meet, it was never enough to get us out of the red.

As a last resort, we even contacted family to see if we could secure a loan, to no avail. I didn't feel comfortable reaching out to my family for two reasons, one, was foolish pride, the other, grief, we had just buried our father. So we embarked on an aspiration that was the epitome of our aberration, (**planning a Bank robbery**)! The day we committed that harrowing act, we had been served a notice of eviction, our power and telephone service was off, and the refrigerator was empty. **Desperation was an understatement!**

> "Hungry men have no respect for law,
> authority, or human life."
>
> MARCUS GARVEY

I could not see my family homeless! This was the statement that kept flashing in and out of my mind like one of those bright neon signs above the Las Vegas strip!

I had to do something! Homelessness in any environment is an unbearable site to behold! And I had never seen homelessness and despair as poignant and commonplace as I witnessed in California! One of the first famous sites that my brother Tony took me to see was Hollywood, Sunset Blvd., and Bel Air. We spent the day there marveling at the beautiful hilltop mansions. All of the expensive sport cars and limousines that traversed the many streets and highways. We visited Mann's Chinese Theater, and the Sidewalks of the Stars. Yet nothing, absolutely nothing, had as much as an impact on my heart and memory as did all of the destitute, homeless people I saw almost everywhere I happened to look! *A Living Paradox!*

"HOMELESS PEOPLE"

Homeless people of every race, running to and fro, so
confused and desperate, nowhere to go!
Shall we sleep here tonight or in a city park? They're eagerly
awaiting the day, to become night's dark!

Mothers and their children are in our streets, no type of
shelter, no running water and no heat!
The Haves have and the Have Nots don't; do you think this
insanity will continue? Guess? It won't!
Just the other day I saw a desperate homeless man, eating
disposed food from a nasty garbage can!
The future is very bleak in our society, if we don't stop this
foolishness right now, immediately!
One of the richest countries on the face of the earth,
we've forgotten what caused its birth!
Why build another missile or another space shuttle, while in the
winter's cold, "**HOMELESS PEOPLE**" huddle!
KBA

The Deputy Sheriff just concluded his arrogant articulation of proper court room etiquette. Everyone began to file into the courtroom. Terri and I seated ourselves up front, while the court calendar was being called. I thought about what a real twist of fate this was for Terri and me. Much of my professional work experience I had been in Public Safety, at the opposite end of the Criminal Justice system.

A Police officer at Georgia State University and Atlanta Police Departments for ten years! A firefighter in Atlanta for a number of years, and the manager of Security at a shopping plaza in Riverside. I had just finished all of the preliminary steps in the hiring process for Riverside County Sheriff's Department. I thought about how blessed we were to come away from this whole ordeal unscathed! I thought about the victims of my crime, how they must have felt with guns displayed openly while my co-defendant and I commandeered that facility!

Weeks before this court date, I did something very unconventional, yet very sincere. I forwarded a detailed letter of apology to all of the staff at that Bank we robbed, acknowledging the error of my ways, and I expressed a renewed commitment to correct the error of my ways while paying my dues to society for my offences. Had I heeded the persuasive power of conscience, I wouldn't be in this courtroom today! I believe it was a ***sign from GOD, HIS grace*** reaching out to me, attempting to save me from my own stupor, my own faults. ***It was a test of my faith, an internal war of good and evil!***

> "Shame arises from the fear of man;
> conscience from the fear of *GOD*."
>
> SAMUEL JOHNSON

In a compelling dream, a very stern, authoritative voice urged me to leave California, not to do what my troubled mind suggested. A premonition urging me to return to Georgia, to my mother, and all of my family there that loved me unconditionally! I awakened the next morning with this dream fresh on my mind, ***every single detail***. I fell victim to the short sighted rational of a man confounded, yet my intuit feelings made me restless, demurred. The powerful presence of **GOD** in me spoke, as **HE** speaks to all of us in so many profound ways! *I heard* **HIM** *loud and clear, but I did not obey* **HIM!**

"IT SPEAKS"
Today that voice within refuses to be silent, ***it speaks***,
then leaves me wondering where it went.

It speaks, about many societies that existed long before all of us.

It speaks, about human love, hate, greed, charity and even trust.

It speaks, about the rich, the poor and mankind's greed and inequality.

It speaks, about mansions, limousines and the ghetto's poverty.

It speaks, about Europe old and new, and many nations fears.

It speaks, about Native Americans, Europeans and the Trail of Tears.

It speaks, about Africa, Mansa Musa, Chaka Zulu, and Timbuktu.

It speaks, about Niggers, Negroes, Blacks, African Americans too.

It speaks, about World Wars 1 and 2, Korea, Vietnam, Iran and Iraq.

It speaks, about all of the monuments where so much youth is plagued.

It speaks, about the Constitution and subsequent laws that prevailed.

It speaks, about the judicial system and
how often justice does fail.

It speaks, about the introduction of an
earthly evil known as crack.

It speaks, about many of the victims who happened to be black.

It speaks, about atheists, believers, gays, lesbians and world religions.

It speaks, about the earth, moon, stars,
sun, mankind and his decisions.

It speaks, about sex, marriage, children,
parents and being alone.

It speaks, to me about those basic principles of right and wrong.
KBA

"My *LORD* forgive and show mercy, for you
are the best of those that show mercy."

QURAN 23:118

As my eyes scanned the courtroom like an oscillating camera, I looked at the disproportionate number of African Americans, Mexicans, Latinos, and other minorities, in proportion to Caucasians, in defendant row, awaiting their names to be called to address some criminal charge against them. It dawned on me in that moment that every court appearance before this one had been exactly this same picture. **How or Why?** I pondered why such a small percentage of the total population in this country was so prominent on this end of the criminal justice system? Were minorities more criminally inclined that arrests, criminal charges and conviction ratios would transcend that of Caucasians, whose numbers comprise about seventy percent of the national population in the United States? *Or was this a sign of that malignant tumor, (racial prejudice), that has tainted race relations in this country since the colonialist days?* Though I accept full responsibility for my actions, it would be unscrupulous not to consider all of the case factors that led me, and possibly many others to the brink of cynicism.

In my sincerest efforts to fix the flaws in my own life, I must leave no stones unturned. A careful perambulation of my whole life, and all of the external influences that impacted it, is a necessary chore. I was born and raised in the South, where the legacy of racism still permeates the very foundations of many communities. The confederate flag that waved boastfully above the Governor's mansion in the State of Georgia until recently, along with the historical plaques and monuments of the pre and post-civil war era that can be found throughout that State and others, are not mere vestiges to be read and viewed by students of history, tourists, and curious onlookers, but are, in fact, *the proud symbols of white supremacists, and their benefactors, (those that benefited from the slave trade), from this savagely cruel, dark and repressive period in American history.*

It wasn't until I relocated to California that *I finally accepted that racism, the false and fragile doctrine of white supremacy,* is indeed a **National Institution**. I thought about all of the experiences of racism that had infected my life from birth until now, from the east coast to the west. The recent loss of employment Terri and I experienced was racially motivated. I had just trained an older white man to be my assistant. He was retired from one employer, boastfully bragging about the pension he receives from that employer. His children were all adults, and he had a bad heart, the recipient one triple by-pass operation already. In that line of work, private security, he should have been denied employment for that reason alone. I know for a fact that any minority candidate certainly would have!

The very same day I was terminated, he was promoted to Director of Security! This was one of the straws that eventually broke the proverbial camel's back! I allowed these experiences of racism to make me cynical and bitter, hostile and suspicious of white people! I walked around with the burden of more than four hundred years of oppression, rape, murder, torture and discrimination inside of me! I knew oh so well about the legacy of racism and the colonialization of the known world by European and American powers, being a student of history since elementary school, and doing my own research when the propaganda we were being taught didn't make sense. I saw and studied so many historic examples of how the American dream had eluded so many for so long in this country! How this land of **milk and honey,** This **"PROMISED LAND,"** had lied, deceived and manipulated my people for over four hundred years!

"PROMISED LAND"

White men declared this land, the **"PROMISED LAND,"**
then recorded that in ink with their blood stained hands!
All men are created equal he openly declared, yet with me
and mine, this true universal precept far often wasn't shared!

He held my ancestors captive to turn his dirty soil, he subjected all of them to bitter hate, and cruel, senseless toil!
He raped girls and women in the open cotton fields, he hung Black boys and men for his entertainment and thrills!
He displayed more compassion for his cats, dogs and horses, our hungry children cried, he ignored their hungry voices!
He had no choice but to eventually remove the shackles and chains, yet continued his plots full of death and pain!
We shall overcome this, we would peacefully sing, then he murdered one of our greatest leaders, the **Dr. King!**
He drafted our youth and shipped them out to fight, yet wouldn't let us vote or enjoy our very basic **human rights**!
Many of my ancestors died, made the ultimate sacrifice, so that their descendants eventually may get just a slice!
Maxine Waters and many others have clear evidence, about placement of drugs and guns in our cities, there is no defense!
Who pardoned the United States for the evil she has committed? If we had a fair trial, would she really be acquitted?
Many Republican administrations, the rich get fatter and fatter, and after all this: we're *screaming* **Black Lives Matter!**
GOD knows you America, your deeds were never veiled, if this ignorance doesn't change America, **you will go to hell!**
KBA

"The problem of the twentieth century is
the problem of the color line."

W. E. B. DUBOIS

The courtroom was eerily silent as the Judge approached the bench. I readjusted my posture in that seat, attempting to focus on the Judge as she prepared to call the cases before her. After the first case was called I took my wallet from my back pocket and placed it inside my jacket pocket. I took my jacket off and gave it to Terri, anticipating my case being called at any time. I leaned over and kissed Terri on her cheek and told her that I love her. I encouraged her to be strong, assuring her that everything would be ok. She told me that she loved me too, that she is mine, and no matter what happens, she will be there for me. The Judge pulled the next case file, looked up and asked if the District Attorney and my attorney were ready to proceed in my case. Butterflies ricocheted off the walls of my stomach as my attorney signaled for me to stand. Terri rose with me. We looked in each other's eyes knowing this was it! I held her close and tight one last time, kissed her again before joining my attorney in front of the Judge's bench. As I stood before the Judge, my mind seemed to go on autopilot, identifying so many clear examples of strength, faith and hope. I thought about my father, Bacadee, his life and influence with me over the years; King David and his Psalms; King Solomon and his Proverbs, and a very special poem through which my **LORD** spoke to me during a period in my life when I was stricken with grief and despair: *I...*

"I"

Take **MY "HAND"** and *"I"* will guide you through, any predicament or trouble you have wandered into!
"I'M THE "KING", "THE MASTER", "THE SOLE RULER OF ALL", next to the highest mountain, *"I"* stand tall!

> *"I"* fixed the moon and stars in their places, ***"I AM"*** the
> ***"SCULPTOR"*** who carved all of your unique faces!
> It is ***"I"*** that allows the sun to shine each day, illuminating the path so you may always find the best way!
> So as you travel that often lonely path, don't pass ***"ME"***
> by, as the wind blows swiftly, don't worry, it is ***"I"!***
> KBA

My attorney appealed to the Judge for leniency in his closing arguments. He asked the Judge to please consider the lowest possible term in my case because of my background, which had no prior convictions, and other unique case factors. The Judge asked if there were any statements or requests I would like to make before the court prior to sentencing, and I said: **no your honor**. Then she said to me: Mr. Akbar, this is what makes my job so difficult!

I have watched you throughout all of these court proceedings, your professional attire, your mannerisms; what appears to be an impeccable background prior to this criminal case. **Perhaps I would rule differently in your case but I can't, because the brand new mandatory minimums, (Strikes law), doesn't give Judges that power anymore!** I looked back at Terri, and at my attorney, and the Judge began to explain the factors she must consider in my case, (intent, malice, the type of crime, my background, etc.), before she pronounces my sentence), **eight years and four months in State prison!** A numbness seized my entire body as I was remanded to custody! The Sheriff's Deputy shackled my hands and my feet and seated me adjacent to the Judge's bench.

Terri squealed the words I love you across the courtroom as tears ran uncontrollably down her face, and I gestured a kiss to her with my lips. She turned and ran out of the courtroom in an emotional tirade! Looking back at me as she stumbled around other people on her way out of that courtroom! I felt so helpless, unable to console her or myself for that matter! In that moment I closed my eyes to the visual reality of my own situation and began to take deep breaths. A few minutes later, the Sheriff's Deputy put me on an automated elevator that led to the basement, where another Sheriff's Deputy was waiting for the elevator to open to receive me, process me, where I would be stripped of all my worldly possessions, and the next few hours would consist of fingerprints, photographs, and disparaging comments and judgements all along the way from the jail staff. I just embarked on my initial trek through this dark and often despondent environment called **County Jail...**

CHAPTER 4

"County Jail"

"Speaking generally, punishment hardens and numbs, it produces concentration, and it sharpens the conscience of alienation, and strengthens the power of resistance."

Friedrich Nietzsche

I WAS PLACED in a dormitory type cell with fourteen other men. This was the old jail with the almost antiquated iron bars all around us, creating a large square as our temporary living quarters. There was one public telephone at the front of the cell that we used alternately, it remained on most of the day. A nineteen inch color television hung high above head for our entertainment, it was bolted in place and offered viewing from most of the networks. Both the telephone and the television could be turned off by the Deputies from a remote switch any time they felt a need to do so.

One toilet and sink sat out in the rear of the cell. On both adjacent walls were bunks stacked four high, welded into each other and the walls. Four metal tables sat in the center of the cell for use at chow time, or any other time we chose to seat ourselves, they were bolted to the floor as well. The showers were situated between two dormitories and the staff allowed us to make use of them on an alternate basis. One dormitory would use the showers in the early part of the day, and the other in the afternoon.

This gave us **inmates** from one dormitory access to the bars of the other dormitory, enabling us the opportunity to interact with other **inmates** at the bars from time to time. Within twenty four hours I had familiarized myself with the routine of things. In our dormitory, the Blacks were the majority. There were Latinos, Mexicans and Whites, Whites being the minority in this case. There are always those in every setting that feel they must be the man, the one in control, **the shot caller**, oppressing the weaker people or least assertive men around them, until they are confronted, then it becomes apparent where their heart really is!

"One man with courage makes a majority".

ANDREW JACKSON

A couple of guys attempted to monopolize the television and the telephone, until they were met with staunch resistance, and they soon conformed. I really had no interest in the television myself, too many thoughts and concerns circulated continuously in my head. The telephone on the other hand was crucial! The distraught image of Terri running out that courtroom crying, laid heavy on my heart and mind! I thought about how my sons must be reacting to the reality that their Daddy is gone for eight years! I thought about Tony, my Mom and the rest of my family and friends that stuck by me regardless of my grievous offence! I had to talk to them, to reassure them that I am ok, that everything is going to be ok! I made several attempts to contact them to no avail. Meanwhile, a rumpus in the adjacent dormitory suggested a situation was developing. I was on the telephone at the time, and I had a clear view into the other dormitory when everyone ran to the bars to see what was going on. *"A fight'! A fight"!* The men uttered around me as I stood with the receiver in my hand! Apparently another conflict over the television.

> "Nine-tenths of the miseries and vices of
> mankind proceed from idleness"
>
> THOMAS CARLYLE

The circumstances surrounding that brawl soon surfaced, the Latinos and Mexicans were unwilling to watch anything except their ethnic programs, and they were the majority in that cell. One of the four Black guys in their dormitory finally had enough, got up and demanded to watch something else. When his demands went unheeded, he began to change the channel himself. He was met with vehement protests!

Then he was surrounded by several Latinos and Mexicans immediately! Only one other Black guy came to his aid when fists began to fly! These two Black guys fought gallantly, fending off ten or more adversaries, while the other two Black guys in that dormitory looked on from the security of their bunks. Blacks in our dormitory shouted strong protests of retaliation into the other dormitory if that lope sided brawl didn't cease immediately! All the other men began to gradually back away as the two Black guys stood courageously with their backs against the bars.

After it was determined that everyone was ok, an internal inquisition was launched amongst the Blacks about the two Black guys that remained on their bunks. Why they didn't help the Black guys that were outnumbered during that Malay? When no real explanation was offered by either one of them, they were ordered to summons the Deputies, to request relocation to another dormitory, or, first opportunity, they could expect a beat down! They signaled for the Deputies by striking their cups against the iron bars.

The Latinos and Mexicans in that other dormitory were admonished contemptuously, and told that if one hair on the head of the two remaining Black guys is harmed, they can expect a full knockdown, drag out riot to jump off as a result of it! The Deputies took the two Black guys to another dormitory, interviewing them along the way, they returned to our dormitories and explained emphatically the County's policy regarding fights and assaults, and promised to come down hard on anyone found in violation of it!

It was this experience in particular that caused me to pay closer attention to the racial make-up and interaction of all the men around me, a necessary survival skill in this volatile environment. Many of us are aware of the racial disparity that has tainted the social fiber of this country from its earliest inception. Yet this was uniquely different, all the rancor and hate of an entire country, compressed tightly into these walls! I watched meticulously as these men of every persuasion walked around with their County jumpsuits pulled down to their waist, displaying the bold inscriptions, (tattoos), proclaiming the prejudices and affiliations of choice; gang; neighborhood; color or ethnicity. There were no limitations or restrictions on their wills to hate!

"Don't hate, it is too heavy a burden to bear."

R℮v. Dr. Martin Luther King Jr.

If the Latinos were not beefing with the Blacks, the Whites were beefing with Latinos, and strangely as it was, the biggest conflicts were with Northern and Southern Latinos and Mexicans. If the Blacks were not busy hating Mexicans, Blacks from the Bloods were warring with Blacks from the Crips, and vice versa! If the Arian brothers and Neo-Nazis were not busy hating Blacks, Latinos and Mexicans, they were beefing amongst themselves! Even these examples haven't been reduced to the least common denominator, it just goes on and on, where it ends, nobody knows! This is symptomatic of a much greater ill. **This is the hate that hate produced!** Where is this ever elusive **Brotherhood of man?**

"BROTHERHOOD"

Why can't we all relate to each like men, love
our fellow man and become true friends?
So much jealousy and unfounded hate, while
time moves swiftly, we all are running late!
Never truly realizing the purpose of our being, traveling through life, open eyes yet unseeing,
To the many degrees of beauty and unlimited love;
it emanates consistently from up above!
So let's love each other and watch love give birth,
to a state of utopia here on this earth!
And by then I am certain that we all really should, have a pure understanding of the word: **"BROTHERHOOD!"**

KBA

Things seemed to settle down in the succeeding hours. This proved to be the foundation to be bring the Blacks together in our dormitory, even if only temporarily.

> "Young single Black men can either represent
> a positive progressive force or one that just
> continues to react to crisis after crisis"
>
> HAKI R. MADHUBUTI

The Black men opened up to each other in our dormitory, expressing their anguish over that racial skirmish, then went on to talk about other concerns or issues of the day. As the conversations between these Black men grew, a symphony of laughter, words, and gestures exploded! I watched as each man took his turn to share his spirited version of life's experiences before incarceration, the author of his own tall tales, to the amusement and entertainment of all those around him! At that moment I thought about how resilient the human spirit really is, how colorfully animated my people really are, and how naturally resourceful we have been and continue to be. The sad fact that the threat or the existence of some sort of crisis with us, had been historically, and still is, our primary rallying call, should draw our attention to the profound lessons of history, in a way that we never forget them!

> "Those that forget the past are destined to repeat it!
> Intellectuals ought to study the past not for the pleasure
> they find in so doing, but to derive lessons from it".
>
> CHEIKH ANTA DIOP

"FROM ME TO YOU"
From beautiful oasis around the Nile Valley: to
Detroit's and Harlem's dead end alleys.
From students of wisdom and beacons of light:
to pimps, thieves, and robbers by night.
From historic cultures and utopian ground: to
white men slave ships westerly bound.
From civilizations of peace, knowledge and love; to
oppression and treachery never thought of.
From degradation and shackles of slavery; to this
era and this generation of you and me.
From here we must do, what we must do, to be free
again, this message is **"FROM ME TO YOU."**
KBA

I became acquainted with one of the two brothers that fought in that confrontation. He was intelligent, charismatic, a small framed man with the heart of a lion. When we were formally introduced, he was overwhelmed by my middle and last name, realizing they were Arabic/Islamic names. He studied Islam previously like I had, and had now committed to realigning himself with its pristine precepts once more. From that point forward, whenever the opportunity presented itself, we would look for each other. We shared and debated personal views and ideas about **GOD,** religion, crime, relationships, children and so on.

It was definitely reassuring, inspiring and even comforting to know how similar our experiences in life were. In spite of the differences in our geographical, social, economic backgrounds, we had a lot in common. We were even convicted of the same crime, **bank**

robbery. He kept expressing a genuine desire to expiate himself before **GOD** while in this state of self-imposed exile, ***incarceration.*** He and I would meet before dawn at the end of the bars to perform prayers together, this was my first collective form of worship behind bars.

We discussed the pillars and articles of our faith, afterwards we would go on to discuss other mundane issues of the day. He told me he was out to court from Federal prison. Apparently he was being questioned about some other unsolved bank robberies. He couldn't understand how or why my case ended up on a State level, when bank robbery is a Federal offence. He said if I had been sentenced to Federal prison, the most I would have done was three and half years on a five year prison term. He felt the State of California had manipulated my case from the Feds to be able to give me more time than the Federal courts would have. He talked about the benefits and amenities offered to ***inmates*** in Federal prison as opposed to State prison. He talked about the huge, expansive libraries; the great educational and vocational programs; the professional demeanor of the staff, the elaborate exercise and weight facilities; the open buffet dining halls, he even told me that cells had carpet on the floor. It seemed strange and eerie, as we sat there weighing the pros and cons of these dark and repressive environments.

I guess this was my earliest acceptance of the fact that I was now property of the State, and I would be for several years to come! He shared his disgust with the squalor and ignorance in the county jail and was very anxious to get back to the Federal prison system. We prayed together for safety and strength, for we knew any day our commitments would lead us in different directions. My third day in the county I was blessed to make contact with my brother Tony and my sons. I knew the news of my sentence weighed heavy on their hearts.

Nonetheless, we rejoiced in that moment, grateful for the opportunity to talk to each other once more, to encourage each other, always! My sons told me that Terri had made arrangements already, for them to visit with me tomorrow. Although I would be excited to see them, I felt embarrassed in a way, for them to see me in here, this way. They also said Terri had taken my sentence really hard, just as I knew she had! They all were doing all that they could to comfort her. I continued even more aggressively, to reach Terri after my conversations with my sons, to no avail. Well, I must see them tomorrow, with my head held high even under these circumstances, even in this environment. I must exude the strength and faith I need them to have!

> "We owe it to ourselves to always look
> on the brighter side of things."
>
> BOOKER T. WASHINGTON

I returned to the territorial security of my bunk. As I sat there, attempting to read the pocket side book I managed to get through all the security check points, the book I had in my suit pocket when I was sentenced, **The Art of Peace, by Morihei Ueshiba**, my mind's eye focused on **Family,** especially Parsons Street, a few blocks from one of the oldest African American Universities in the country, **Atlanta University Center.** This is where my father and his siblings were raised, where my grandmother, Cora Beavers, (known to all of us as Na-Na), lived and died at age 94, and my uncle Neal, who took care of his mother there until her death. My father had two older sisters too, (Thelma and Ethel), and he was the youngest of them all. .I never got the chance to know my grandfather, (Arthur David Beavers Sr.), he died before I was born. I thought about all of the wonderful dinners we had there, and the swinging outdoor sofa that hung from an old oak tree in the front yard, and soon that book, bunk and cell became evanescent.

"FAMILY"

Holding loving communions on a regular basis, trying to compensate for lost time and spaces.
Reflections of experiences when we were all small, how some of us were short, and some tall.
Reflections of a love that is always openly displayed, an oath of love that must never be betrayed!
A beautiful mother and father from which we came, qualities in them and all of us are the same.
I have so many relatives, all beautiful in their own right, and I love each of you with all of my might!
Though I wish, our destinies I can't really see, I pray that all of you feel this love coming from me!
And may **GOD** grant true faith to all of us, for there is prosperity if in **HIM** we all continue to trust.
And together we will all grow like a giant oak tree, this is my experience and perception of the word: **"FAMILY."**
KBA

Dedicated to the love and memory of Cora and Arthur David Beavers Sr.

Those of us already **convicted** of our crimes in the county jail were simply waiting for the next bus to **State prison.** I've been told by the many **recidivists** I encountered in the county jail that State prison will be a lot better than these present conditions are. That State prison is where you have some structure, and you will be able to **program.** What that means I do not have a clue? Yet I find myself anxious to find out! These deplorable conditions here, and the volatile young men in county jail makes this a vicarious situation.

I watched many young men come here with a mere nine months to do, and they end up going back to court because they got into a fight for whatever the reason was, and they ended up with a three year stint in **State prison.** So for many reasons, I found myself ready to go to the next level, even though I knew nothing about what really awaited me there.

> "You gain strength, courage, and confidence by each experience in which you stop to look fear in the face. You are able to say to yourself, I have lived through this horror. I can take the next thing that comes along. You must do the thing you cannot do."
>
> ELEANOR ROOSEVELT

I did have valid concerns that could not be discounted. My first good job in California was in Security. At one of the malls in Riverside. When I took that job, the demographics were that this mall was surrounded by gang infested communities and other errant youth. They terrorized the customers and shop owners alike. So my first challenge was to make this a safe place to shop. So I increased security outside the mall. Then I created a bicycle patrol for the parking lots and parking deck, so we could maneuver around moving and parked cars quickly, when necessary.

For the next ninety days, Riverside Police were always at the mall, picking up individuals we had detained for shoplifting and other offenses. My personal efforts in this capacity sent a number a people to jail. I was surprised I had not encountered any of these individuals in the county jail, or had they already been sent to State prison, and now I would be readily identified by them when I get off the bus. What would the State prison system really be like? How would **inmates** be housed and segregated in the next facility called **State prison?**

Where would this **State prison** be located? For there are many throughout Northern and Southern California, and I was informed early on by my attorney, that I could be transferred to any one of them: **remanded to the State, State property**. As I pondered these, and other matters of the heart, I laid back, closed my eyes and began to meditate on the **LORD,** believing that all of **HIS PROMISES** are true; that **HE** really is omniscient, so even in this place, on this day, **HE** is present with me. I dozed off to sleep with this calming energy, and I awakened to this one: *"KEEP YOUR FOCUS!"*

"KEEP YOUR FOCUS"

As we embark on our journeys in life, there are things we all must do, I pray for words of wisdom right now, for me and all of you.
I stood alone in quiet darkness, and pleaded with
GOD for **HIS light,** for the true knowledge of
JESUS and **KING SOLOMAN'S** insight.
Then in a matter of a few seconds, there appeared a light on the wall, there were vivid images of me and they told it all.

As I stood there trembling with fear, too afraid to look away, I
heard a stern voice call out my name, here's what **HE** had to say:
You've had the benefit of Church; Mosque, study,
and many years of life, **I'VE** walked with you, and
I carried you often, through joy and strife!
Although you've turned your back on **ME, I'VE**
kept a watchful eye on you, when you fell to your
knees in prayer, *I* came to see about you!
While in meditative prayer, now *I AM* responding to your call, *I* came to see you **PERSONALLY**,
I put all those images on the wall!
This is what *I* require of you: prayer, faith, fasting, charity and good deeds, fight against the sinful ways of man, plant brand new spiritual seeds!
This is the way to salvation, stay away from the devil's hocus pocus, and *I* will bless you on earth and
heaven, if you just **"KEEP YOUR FOCUS!"**
KBA

"And *HE* is with you wherever you are."

Quran 57:4

"Have I not commanded you? Be strong and courageous.
Do not be afraid; do not be discouraged; for the *LORD*
your *GOD* will be with you wherever you go."

Joshua 1:9

I was startled awake by the very authoritative voice in the dark of night, a Deputy Sheriff said Kenneth Bilal Akbar, roll it up, you're leaving! It had to be around two in the morning. As I gathered myself and then my sheets and blankets to drop in a bin outside the cellblock, as instructed, I knew that this was it, I'm about to take that ride to **State prison.** Several of us filed out of open cellblock doors into a very well-lit area, where we were corralled together, and then escorted downstairs via the elevator to more Deputies and shackles lined up against the walls.

Once the walls were lined up with **inmates** from one end of the corridors to the other, we were told to turn around and face the walls, then, Deputies systematically shackled us, ankles and wrists, and then one to another, in a way that ensured we surely could not run because you could not walk without jerking and causing pain to your wrists and ankles if our movements were not synchronized! Some of us had to insist that the shackles were too tight and they needed to be readjusted! The large garage type door rose, and the smell of carbon monoxide filled the air from the giant bus that was running, waiting for all of us to board.

Group by group, shackled three by three, we boarded that bus, and we had do this sideways, for the shackles would not cooperate any other way! Once we were all on board, one Deputy stepped into a black, reinforced cage facing us, where he picked up a loaded shotgun, inspected it, and another began to explain to all of us the rules of the road aboard this bus before we embarked on this journey to the unknown. As the bus pulled out of the jail complex and I could began to see streets and other cars and the sights of the civilized world I was about to leave behind, I cried and smiled internally at the same time.

I was delighted to see the real world after experiencing the drudgery of County jail, yet I was saddened by the realization that I was about to leave all of this and so much more behind for a very long time! As the bus sped down local roadways to get to the main highways, I took it all in, for who knew if, or when, I would ever see it again! As the bus hit dips and bumps in the road, the tightened shackles seem to tighten up on their own as we jolted and readjusted to those violent, unexpected occurrences.

And any legitimate, real cry of pain or frustration because of it was met by strict guidelines of no outcries or outbursts will be tolerated on this bus! After about an hour of travel, the Deputies asked if any of us needed to use the restroom, and if so, you must acknowledge this right now, so they could systematically release us from one another so this could be accomplished, before they passed out sack lunches to all of us. The sack lunches consisted of one dry peanut butter and jelly sandwich on white bread, one apple and a child size carton of milk. **When food is scarce, even the worse food can seem quite delicious…**

> "If we were really tough on crime, we'd try to save
> our children from the desperation and depravation
> that leave them primed for a life of crime."
>
> CARRIE P. MEEK

As we maneuvered through that mountainous terrain, I felt a chill come over me, a physiological chill that I felt in the recesses of my soul. As the bus came over the last peak, there it stood, nestled away in between mountains, a massive complex, with various buildings sprawled out over acres and acres of land, with double perimeter gates that stood so high they couldn't be scaled, with barbed wire fixed at the highest point, double wrapped! We were in the mountains of Tehachapi, **Tehachapi State prison.**

"WHAT A PRICE TO PAY!"

Emotions and passions untamed, led me impetuously, obstinately denying that anything was wrong with me.
Fast cars, fast women, drugs and alcohol use, I didn't know that these pleasures would lead to a life of abuse.
Buried animosity and hostility, a legacy of pain, racial strife, child abuse, a life that anyone would come to disdain.
No counseling, no therapy, a child ready to explode, looking to someone, somewhere to dump this heavy load.
Now here I am years later, arriving at State penitentiary, sentenced to an eight year term before I will be free.
About to face the chaos of prison life, day by day, and the absence of all my liberties, **"WHAT A PRICE TO PAY!"**

KBA

"If my people, which are called by **MY NAME**, shall humble themselves, and pray and seek **MY FACE,** and turn from their wicked ways; then will *I* hear from heaven, and will forgive their sin, and will heal their land."

CHRONICLES 7: 14

"For the **LORD** hears the needy and does not despise **HIS** own people who are prisoners."

ISIAH 6: 11

CHAPTER 5

"STATE PRISON"

"Lock up your libraries if you like; but there is no gate,
no lock, and no bolt that you can set upon my mind."

VIRGINIA WOOLF

AS THE BUS came to a stop adjacent to one of the buildings, a large sign read: **Tehachapi State Prison Reception Center.** Both deputies exited the bus and walked into the building. They were gone for almost thirty minutes before they returned to the bus and began to systematically remove us from the bus, row by row. As I stepped off that bus into the early morning air, along with the two men I was shackled to, an eerie realization came over me, this is the beginning of a very long journey! We were escorted into the building where more officers awaited us, with night sticks in hand, they uttered instructions to all of us: Line up against that wall, where the shackles were removed.

Once the shackles were removed, we were told to take off all of our clothing, and leave them on the floor, we were lined up and assigned officers one on one, and they searched every nook and cranny, all hidden recesses of our bodies were searched, and then we were required to bend over and cough several times, to dislodge any and all *contraband that inmates smuggle into these places*. Then we were all placed in a holding cell in our **birthday suits, butt naked!**

We were packed into that holding cell to the extent that one could not avoid bumping into each other as we attempted to reposition ourselves. As I stood there in that holding cell, I noticed there was a large sign beneath the *gun tower* in Spanish and English which read: **No Warning Shots Will Be Fired,** and a gun barrel protruded from the gun port at the top of the tower in our direction manned by another officer. One by one, they called us out of that holding cell by name, gave us our first State issue, which consisted of a pair of white boxers, one pair of white socks, one white T-shirt, cloth, flat soled shoes and an orange jump suit.

We were returned to that holding cell where we were given sack lunches again. After many of the *inmates* consumed their sack lunches, they found places on the floor to lie down, for many of them this was not a new experience, and they knew it would be hours before the officers would revisit us again. Hours later, tables were set up where civilian prison staff laid out blank documents, then they sat on one side of the table. The officers returned and began to call us out by name to have a seat on the other side of the table where we were processed.

The civilian prison staff asked us medical questions, background information, educational background and work history. Out of all the questions that were asked, the one that caught me off guard, and caused me to squirm in my seat, was this one: ***Should you die in here, who should we contact***? I looked at that man wide eyed and replied: ***I'm not dying in here!*** The man that posed the question looked at me with a smirk on his face and said: ***I still need that information before we can proceed.***

I gave him my Brother Tony's information, reluctantly! Once that process was completed, we were given clean sheets and a blanket and assigned to cells with bunk beds bolted to the walls, my cell was upstairs. I was instructed to walk up to that cell door, once I arrived, an officer popped it open remotely and I walked inside and closed the door behind me. The other **inmate** already asleep in the lower bunk, had taken pieces of cardboard and placed them in the one window that would allow sunlight to come through, and he had done the same thing to the small glass window on the cell door, so once the cell door was shut, you couldn't see your hand in front of your face!

I used my hand to find the bunk frame, where I maneuvered my way in the dark, up onto that top bunk. There I sat in utter darkness, motionless, as the whole experience of being processed into the State system, replayed itself over and over inside my head. After sitting there in darkness for a while, it got cold fast, and I realized that I needed to make this bed and get under these sheets and covers, and the only way I can see to do that was to remove the cardboard from the door, at least. So that's what I did.

When I turned around, there stood a man with a dark complexion, and long black hair laid down behind his head like Blackula! The light from the door illuminated his visage and it resembled black and white TV! And he said: Hey man! I'm trying to get some sleep if you don't mind! And I replied: How do expect me to make my bunk in the dark? I thought so! Then I handed him the cardboard while I began to make my bunk. He stood there waiting impatiently, waiting for me to finish, and once I did I said: My name is Ken Akbar by the way, and he, with his back to me, bumbled out: Harold, as he repositioned the cardboard back into place, and the cell went dark again.

"Better to light a candle than to curse the darkness."

Chinese Proverb

So I left that alone, and pursued the best course, get myself in a defensive posture up here on this bunk, one where I can see and feel, even as I rest. And I found it, my feet at the cell door and head against the wall. I can pounce from here like the lion that I am, if and when necessary! From this bird's eye view, this comfort zone, I began to doze off. The awakening at the County jail, and processing there, then the long and arduous road trip shackled, and the staging and processing here had taken its toll on me, and I was exhausted!

So off I went to that other space, of repose, even here. After several hours, I was awakened to a loud chatter by my cellmate screaming expletives through a vent near the toilet that connected to other cells and could be heard from someone he knew or had become acquainted with since arriving here, who knows? What I do know is I can see early on that this man and I are going to need to have some face to face time about basic etiquette! What are the rules we both can mutually honor and respect in here together, however long we may be here together! So I allowed him to continue his very disruptive dialogue with whomever, for a while

After this continued for some time, I sat up on my bunk in sheer disgust, as I peered down on his head while he spoke into that vent like it was a microphone! A few minutes later, there was a stirring, I could hear it outside the cell door. And it was obviously a familiar sound to Harold, because he turned to me and said: They are about to bring us lunch, and I do trade items, I said: Fine, thanks for letting me know. We were on the second tier so it would be a few minutes before they arrived with hot lunches in a push cart. So I laid back on my bunk and took it all in, with the lights now on, and the cardboard out of the window and the door, sunlight beaming through, I could see that there was a nature reserve right outside that window, **untamed!**

Eagles, Hawks, and Falcons, soaring above head, because in that pristine environment I been placed in, it wasn't man in control at all, but **GOD!** Vultures circling above head too, scanning the ground and patiently awaiting whatever is left over for them, after the fresh feast! I could see dear and skunks, squirrels and chipmunks, and different species of wild pigeons! And Bobcats flourished on the smaller prey! Coyotes and Wolf too!

> "The weak die out, and the strong will
> survive, and will live on forever."
>
> ANNE FRANK

They did finally arrive with our hot lunches which consisted of crashed potatoes, suffocated chicken and mean beans, plus stone bread! And I dispatched as much of that as I could tolerate without vomiting, then I resolved myself to settle down in my own self-inflicted circumstance and condition. Yet be sure to keep my eye on the primary goal, and that it is, to get back to all those that mean the world to me in the world, in spite of my own stupidity!!!

> "Two things are infinite, the universe and human stupidity; and I'm not sure about the universe."
>
> ALBERT EINSTEIN

Later in the afternoon, an officer could be heard on the lower tier calling out **CDC numbers,** all **inmates** that have been processed into the State system will be assigned **California Department of Corrections and Rehabilitation numbers**, which began with an alphabet, and a photo identification card; with this number on it will follow you when you **parole** back to the streets of society. That officer was doing the mail run, approaching each cell door and sliding mail to the appropriate recipients. As his voice yelled out names and numbers, something unusual began to happen between my cellmate and me.

    He began pacing the cell floor, from one end to the other, pausing at times to glare out the narrow glass window on the cell door. He got really anxious and opened up to me all of sudden about his family, his wife and kids. How he had fathered eight kids with a woman that had seen him through three prison terms over the years. How he hoped today would be the day that he would receive some kind of correspondence from them. He had been in reception here for four weeks and had not received anything. He seemed really worried, so I offered some encouragement and said maybe this will be the day that you hear from them. What he told me next caused me to sit on the edge of my bunk! You don't know what happened man, why I'm in here right now! You're right, I retorted.

I jumped on her man! I beat her up pretty bad too man! I'm in here for domestic violence, they charged me with aggravated battery against a spouse! I can do five years behind that charge! The crazy thing is I love that woman, she just kept interfering with one of my hustles, getting in between me and my **hoes**. **She knows I been pimping and selling drugs for years!** My hair don't look like this by accident, this shit cost money to maintain! He pointed at the pictures of his wife and kids on the table and mentioned how much he missed them, as I sat on the edge of my bunk with my mouth agape!

I thought about all those Foxy Brown and Superfly movies I grew up watching in the seventies! This is nineteen ninety five! This man was as proud of that as if he were an accomplished artist or pianist, as he began to name the women, describe their features, and ethnicity to me. That's when I said whoa my man! Are you listening to yourself at all? Well I listened attentively to everything you just said, and you lost me somewhere in the opposite extremes of your own life! Ok, let me share some things with you about me: I have never been to prison before, this is my first time, and I'm determined to make it my only time!

I believe that the only way that has a chance at all to come true, is I, you, or anyone else for that matter, needs to really look at what went wrong, what led us here in the first place! You sitting down there on that toilet bragging to whomever that is that's listening on the other end about how many hoes you had and the big drug deals you've sponsored seems counterproductive, and it's very rude and disruptive! **Nobody wants to hear that mess, especially me!** Here's some advice to you: If you really are tired of coming back and forth to these places, and you want your family back, change your ways while you're here this time. About that time the officer was two cell doors down, and Harold took his attention away from me and looked at the door intently! The officer walked right pass our door, no mail. Harold looked at me in dismay, then laid on his bunk and covered himself up completely, including his head. I began to read the only literature that I still had, **The Art of Peace.**

> "Each one of us has to find his peace from within. And peace to be real must be unaffected by outside circumstances."
>
> MAHATMA GANDHI

Later in the evening, the staff made an announcement on the intercom that chow/dinner will be ready to be served in an hour, that each dorm will be escorted to the main chow hall in numerical order, (dorms 1, 2, 3, etc..).. I looked down underneath my bunk at my cellmate, and he was still covered, so I left him alone for a while. Thirty minutes later, the announcement said, dorm three, get ready for chow. I looked down at my cellmate again, and this time I called out his name, Harold, are you going to chow? He said: n'all, I aint going. I said ok, then I got down from my bunk and washed up. I sat on the metal stool which is welded to the metal table in the back of the cell.

Twenty minutes later, the cell door popped open, we were instructed to step out of the cell and shut the cell door behind us. Then we were instructed to file down in an orderly fashion tier by tier. Once we were all lined up, the door leading outside our dorm slid back hydraulically, and officers in front of us, behind us, and adjacent to our flanks said lets go, stay in line, and no talking to and from chow! It was a brisk evening, not too cold, yet a winter chill filled the air. We walked in single a file to the chow hall, where we lined up to receive trays and plastic forks and knives. Then we walked past the serving area where other *inmates* served us the items on our trays.

Then we sat, with fifteen minutes to consume our dinner. At the fifteen minute mark, an alarm type bell sounded and we were instructed to stand, right now, done or not! We were told to place trays and plastic forks and knives in the huge containers on our way out of the chow hall. We were escorted back to our dorm and back into our cells, the same way that we left them. My cellmate was still underneath the covers. The fresh winter air did me some good, more so than the food. I continued reading my little book until I dozed off to sleep. The next morning, around six o clock, the announcement came over the intercom, dorm three, breakfast will be served in thirty minutes. I sat up, got down off my bunk and washed up.

Breakfast and lunch are served to us in our cells, dinner is the only time we get escorted to the chow hall. My cellmate laid there motionless, and once again, I asked if he was going to eat breakfast, and he replied: n'all man, then rolled over on his side. I was starting to believe that the stress of the situation with him and his family was starting to take its toll on him, refusing to eat, and staying underneath his covers and all. After breakfast, I, along with other *inmates* that had just arrived at the reception center, had to go for educational equivalency testing and medical exams on the other side of the prison yard.

The very first stop was with the ***doctors, more like quacks***, at the medical infirmary. This doctor was an old white man that seemed to need a doctor himself! His hands shook as he sat me down and began to examine my ears, eyes, nose, throat and mouth like he was inspecting me prior to auction. He took my blood pressure, pulse, and asked me a battery of medical questions about me and my family. Then he put on latex gloves, asked me to stand and drop my pants.

He examined my testicles like they were coconuts on a tree, then instructed me to bend over and spread my cheeks. Now this is where I resisted, and asked *why, may I ask please?*

He informed me that he needed to check my prostate gland, so bend over, he said a little more assertively, I complied. Thank **GOD** the man had small hands, because you would have thought he had lost something up my ass! *Hey! Hey*! I said several times before he instructed me to turn my head to the right, and then to the left while coughing, before he removed his hand from my anus! I was glad that was done, and I determined myself in that moment to never see that man, *doctor,* ever again! Once a number of us were done with the medical assessments, we were escorted to a classroom type setting, with the old style desks we used in elementary school.

We were instructed to have a seat, filling each row of desks. I felt my behind throbbing as I sat down on that old wooden desk. Other *inmates* brought us pencils, test booklets, and answer sheets. Then the civilian prison staff stepped in and gave us all the instructions we needed to follow while taking this exam, which included this statement: *Should any of you score below a ninth grade education, by law, in the State of California, we are required to place you in school while here.* We were given an hour to take this test which consisted of math problems, reading comprehension, and other problem solving type scenarios. By the time we all finished, it was almost lunch time, so we were escorted back to our dorms and cells. Upon entering that cell, I found Harold up, sitting on the toilet, talking to someone through the vent again.

I climbed up onto my bunk and attempted to tune him out. This effort became harder and harder as he got louder and louder! Rehearsing that ignorance, the evil and crimes that brought him to prison in the first place! Bragging about the money he made, and hoes he pimped! I was incensed! Seething inside like a pressure cooker with no steam relief valve! Thank **GOD** they had reached our tier with lunch, so he and the other idiot could cease with the rhetoric and prepare to have some lunch! After lunch, they had us gather all of our dirty sheets, boxers, T-shirts and socks, and toss them outside the cell door, where other ***inmates*** came around with large push carts and gathered the dirty stuff, then they returned fifteen minutes later with clean stuff. An announcement was made informing us they we will be allowed to shower in an hour, section by section, tier by tier....I was really excited about taking a hot shower, finally

"An existence deprived of freedom is a kind of death."

MICHAEL AOUN

I took note of the fact that Harold did not come out to shower; an odor has already staled the air in that prison cell. In close quarters with one another like that, even for a short period of time, is enough time for germs and bacteria to get transferred, from one to another. ***This is real!*** I'm taking note of certain adjustments I must make in this sojourn going forward. I must be the stronger presence in any cell going forward now, and demonstrate and demand the highest standards of personal hygiene in there! I must also, control the energy in any cells going forward. I must turn this cell into my personal cocoon, my only refuge away from the insanity of prison life! The **LORD** has already given me so many affirmations that **HE** is with me, even in here! I must use my time in here to make myself stronger than ever before! Make myself a *"NEW MAN."*

"NEW MAN!"

I'm going to a place that is afar, just beside the brightest of star.
To let its light shine all over me, illuminating my soul tremendously.
Transforming my heart and my mind; leaving that old shell behind!
A **"NEW MAN"** like never before, energies flowing in me forever more!
If by fate we see each other again, you won't know me because I'll be a:
"NEW MAN!"
KBA

I need to ask where I can get cleaning products for the toilet and sink. And I must have that talk with my cellmate, the sooner the better. The familiar sounds of the mail being distributed on the lower tier, roused Harold off his bunk, and once again, he began his nervous pace, back and forth in that cell. Now, it's progressed to bumbled jargon under his breath as he paced back and forth nervously. I looked down at that concrete floor and noticed for the first time that there was a runway formed in that concrete from *inmates* pacing back and forth over time.

As the officers arrived on our tier, Harold froze facing the door, in hopeful anticipation that a letter or two would be slid under the door for him, and when they walked by our cell door, Harold's shoulders dropped, as if he had been completely deflated of air. He spun around with his head down, and dived on his bunk, then screamed in anguish! I laid back on that bunk and found myself trying to make some real sense of this dilemma for him. One part of me felt sorry for him, another part of me didn't! No real remorse or penitence; yet very strong hopes or expectations for a situation he caused. Over the next three days, this vicious cycle with Harold only got worse!

No mail, no chow, no shower....I watched this man's hair began to grey right before my eyes! Today, is the day. I asked Harold to sit up on his bunk while I sat on the stool. I began to share my observations with him about his behaviors, and how they have a direct bearing on me in these close quarters like this, and I can't go another day with things being as they are in this cell! Then I told him at the rate he is going, he is going to make himself sick before he even gets out of this reception center, and me too, if he doesn't start showering!

I explained to him that I know I've been very tolerant of his behaviors so far, but the train stops here today, and if he has a problem with what I said, there are two options: **1.** Request to be reassigned to another cell, or, **2.** Comply with what I requested. Harold said ok, and laid back down. The very next day, when the mail ran and he didn't get mail, he lost it! He starting screaming and kicking the door, crying uncontrollably! The officer passing out the mail came back to our cell door and waved for the officer in the tower to pop open our cell door, and when he did, Harold ran out of the door screaming and shouting incoherent words and statements! The officers had to run him down and subdue him! They hog tied him and carried him away to ***administrative segregation, (Adseg)…***

"MUSTARD SEED"

A wretched state, tormented human lives; separated from all
their children and their wives.
Locked down! Loss of freedom is the price! For a life full
of worldly pleasures and avarice.
Distracted by card games, chess, and dominoes; volatile mood
swings subject to the mail flow.
Nightmares of her in another man's arms; symptoms of an
insecure man, now he is very alarmed!
Frantic phone calls to dispel this belief; these concrete walls
are cold, can't seem to find relief!
How could she do this to me? Man, I'm through! Walking
around up tight, I'll put hands on you!
Forcefully handcuffed; he's headed to Adseg! He resists their
authority, so they hog tie both his legs!
In solitude these thoughts are still there, he begs **GOD** on his
knees to please make them disappear!
To himself he begins a neurotic converse, days turn into nights,
and his condition gets far worse!
Officers at his cell door, in his present state he can't figure
them out; your mail came in reroute.
The stress was too much, he's lost inside his own head; the
doctors decide to prescribe for him: hot meds!
His perfumed, postmarked letters speak to all of us; what
is a man without constancy and trust?

The moral of this story I hope we will all heed: Mountains can be moved with the faith of a **"MUSTARD SEED!"**
KBA

After things settled down, I thought about how tragic that whole situation was, and, on the brighter side of things, I have the cell to myself for now. And anybody that comes into close quarters with me from now on must know what the rules are! After nearly two weeks in reception now, the officers made an announcement one sunny morning in Tehachapi, that, all of us would be allowed to go out to the prison yard for the very first time. To walk the track around the yard, whatever. The only caveat to this is, once you go out, you must remain on the yard for the entire duration of the yard time, under no circumstance will anyone be allowed to go in and out, albeit, emergencies.

    I pondered this far awhile…We had not yet been issued coats, necessary gear in Tehachapi! Although it was a beautiful morning, approaching afternoon, I had my own reservations. After more deliberation, I decided to take the risk. I mean, what can happen in one hour? We all lined up and awaited the officer to hit the switch for the door to open to the yard. As that door opened and I began to step outside, something inside me said turn around and run back to your cell! I ignored it, and walked out onto the yard reluctantly. And it was truly a glorious day in Tehachapi! The air was so fresh and crisp! Picturesque, snowcapped mountains in the background; birds of every species circling overhead! Thick forestry running up and down this rich, pristine region; there were bears and mountain lions up there in those mountains.

We walked the track, got on the basketball court and played some ball, I sat out and marveled at the sheer beauty of this nature reserve! After nearly forty minutes on the yard, the winds began to blow more forcefully, then, dark clouds began to blow overhead in a matter of minutes, then, it began to rain, then, it began to sleet, and the temperature dropped by ten degrees in five minutes! We all began to make our way to the dorm door as weather conditions continued to worsen. Then all of sudden, the winds picked up and it began to snow. I would say we had twenty minutes left on our yard time and the officers would not let us in until that time had completely expired! As conditions worsen fast, with no coats in this type of weather, we were in trouble! We all yelled while pointing at the gun tower and the officers came over the intercom system laughing, saying welcome to Tehachapi! We will not open that door until your yard time has completely expired, remember that! We had to huddle together in that in climate weather for the last ten minutes of our yard time! When that door finally began to open, we were in before it opened completely!

"The cold can cut like a many knifed blade."

ISRAEL ZINGWILL

This is when I learned that I was really at home in these mountains. This was once the land of Native Americans for centuries, before the European occupation. I have prominent Native American blood in me. Tehachapi is a Native American word that means the place of many seasons, *in the same day!* . **(Smile).** We were allowed yard time every day after this incident, and I was issued a coat for the cold weather. As I spent time on the yard, I stood in the shadows of the activity, and watched as other **inmates** already processed and endorsed to this level, which is level three, there are four levels at this facility. Level four being the highest custody, and level one being minimum level custody.

They were dressed in prison blues, a long sleeve light blue shirt, navy blue Dickie type slacks, and prison boots. I noticed that some of these guys even had uniforms creased and boots polished, military style. I watched as they went in and out of the other three dorms almost at will. The officers would wait sometimes until a number of them had gathered at the door before opening it. I learned these **inmates** were called **pwc's**, which stands for **prison work camp**. After returning to the dorm, I reviewed some of the paperwork I had been given by the civilian prison staff during orientation, Title 15, the booklet with all of the rules and regulations governing permissible prison behavior, and parole as well.

I could hear the familiar sound of mail being distributed in the background as I continued to review this booklet. Before long, an officer was at my cell door, called my name, and then required me to call out my CDC number before sliding my mail under the door. It was a large envelope that was used to send this package express mail. I looked at the sender's information and it was from my brother Tony. I opened the package and found a small sheet of paper with these words written on it by my brother.

Black, (a nickname my two younger brothers and I use to greet each other), How are you doing my brother? I trust and pray that you're remaining strong and faithful. I thought long and hard about whether I should tell you this right now or not, I realized that I had to. The boys moved out of my house and moved in with a family called the Luginbills. They got really confrontational with me after you left. I couldn't talk to them anymore without an argument. I'm sorry bro! I haven't met this family yet, their son goes to high school with the boys. I love you man! Miss you already! I dropped that envelope and letter on the floor and fell to my knees!

Right there and then, I pleaded with the **MASTER, THE SOVEREIGN RULER OF ALL THINGS**, to please watch over my sons, my brother and his family, and all of my family while I'm away. I learned early on in this prison experience that your influence or role in the family doesn't stop because you go away like this. To the contrary, it becomes apparent what can happen in the absence of it! After chow that evening, I returned to my cell and read myself to sleep. While asleep, I had a *night visitor,* he said his name was *"GABRIEL"*...

"GABRIEL"

Have you heard the sounds of a very sick infant cry?
Have you seen any addicted youth gradually die?
Have seen the young people rob and beat the old?
Have you seen the corners where virginity is sold?
Have you heard the screams of a woman being raped?
Have you seen the ghettos where poverty is draped?
Have you heard about the wars in the Middle East?
Have you seen the mad search for the Mengele beast?
Have you taken a real, very careful look all around?
Have you heard the **Angels trumpets sound?**

KBA

After five weeks in reception, I was called out of my cell and given a pass by one of the officers to go see the civilian prison staff about placement; where I would be endorsed to go, which prison facility and where. It was the same guy that interviewed me early on in this process. I waited outside his area until he saw me seated and called my name, and I replied: yes. He said come and have a seat. He began by saying that because of my commitment offenses, I will never be allowed to get minimum security clearance, I will always be at level three or higher, and that I have been endorsed to remain here at Tehachapi, level three, and I can anticipate being moved within a week or so.

That I will be called out before that and provided with my State issue, (pants, shirts, boots, skull caps, and a better coat, plus new socks, T-shirts, boxers and linen) I didn't know what to think about being endorsed to stay here, yet nothing can be done about it so I must roll with the program. Upon returning to my cell I noticed before the cell door was popped open that I had a new cellmate. I walked in and he stood up and introduced himself, Charles, he told me that he preferred to be called Chuck. I introduced myself and sat down to speak with this young man for a while. He told me what he had been convicted of, how much time the courts had given him, and where he hoped to go serve his time.

Chuck was originally from the Bay area, (Oakland), and hoped to be transferred to a facility near that area. It became apparent early on that Chuck was another *recidivist*, having gone back and forth, in and out these facilities for years. I gave Chuck a little information about me, and explained to him that I have already been endorsed to stay here. **His initial reaction to me being endorsed to remain here left an indelible impact on me! You don't want to** *stay up here man! Trust me! It's cold up here a lot, and the officers up here are colder! Straight racist man! Then the coldest of it all is this, you are probably going to end up in the PIA, (Prison Industry Authority).*

Naturally I asked what is the prison industry authority? He began to explain to me that here at Tehachapi, there is a very large factory where furniture is manufactured by the inmates, which are called pwc's. He further stated that when you start in that factory, you must sand a minimum of four chairs a day, by hand, with no gloves! In a few days your fingertips will be so sore, red and swollen, you won't be able to write letters. If you don't make that daily quota, you risk being wrote up and getting sent to the hole, Adseg! It's nothing but a slave camp! The way they talk to you and treat you in that factory is criminal, and these sadistic officers up here love it!

You can file paperwork with your counselor, explaining that it will be a greater hardship on you and your family if you remain up here, so you request to be transferred to another prison like Chino or Indio, closer to Riverside. I thanked Chuck for this insightful information, and I would be less than honest if I didn't say that some of the things Chuck shared with me did leave me with concerns. I prayed over them and went on with my day. A few days later, I was called out of my cell and given a pass to go and pick up my State issue. I went out on the yard and approached windows like those you would see at a hamburger stand that only has outdoor seating.

I gave the guy on the other side of the window by slip, then he began to ask me my shoe size, pants size, shirt size and boxer size. Within minutes he began to hand me all of my stuff, he even gave me a brand new coat still in the plastic. I walked back to the dorm with all of this stuff in my arms and upon returning to my cell, my cellmate decided to throw some cynicism, humorously. They must really need some new strong bodies for the factory! Ha. Ha. Ha….After chow that evening, Chuck and I talked for a while. I don't remember how we ended up talking about child abuse, I'm certain that he brought the subject up. He let me know that he had been a victim of child abuse.

He told me that his mother really did love his father, even though he was a player. That he was the only child his father had with his mother. That because he looked just like his father, his mother would turn her scorn toward his father onto him. That his mother would lock him in closets for days! That she would burn him with cigarettes, and deprive him of food and water for days! Chuck told me he never ended up in Foster care, and when he became a teenager, he began to rebel against his mother and took to the streets, where he encountered gangs, violence and drugs! He told me all of this because he still has nightmares about those horrors, and then he asked had I heard him before now screaming or talking in his sleep, and if so, that's what it is due to!

Chuck's disclosure seemed too genuine to dismiss, and caused me to think about how many of us in these institutions are really just damaged goods, victims of horrible childhood experiences that left us impaired and too dysfunctional to fit into the norms of society? Later in the early morning, as Chuck and I slept, it happened! Chuck began to talk in his sleep as if he was having conversation with someone, then he began shaking violently, then he began to scream! I jumped down off my bunk and said Chuck, Chuck, it's just a dream, it's alright, and it's just a dream! He awakened and shook his head several times and said he had a massive headache.

He apologized for the disruption, and within ten minutes he was already back asleep. It wasn't that easy for me though, I lay awake for some time, wide awake, and my energy and thoughts transcended these prison walls. I thought about all of the strife; wars; all of the abuse and cruelty from man to his fellow man. I thought about all the greed and poverty in the world today, because we have been regulated to following **man's plan** and not the **"MASTER'S PLAN"**...

"MASTER'S PLAN"

These energies are flowing a thousand miles an hour, I'm
trying to understand the purpose of all this power!
Compelling me to search my soul, inside and out, to realize my true dreams and their whereabouts!
Visions that are so beautiful, far from common sight,
but for some this vision shines very, very bright.
Those whose perspectives that are keen and aware,
can the magnitude of this poetic writing truly share.
The full beauty and power that is within our hands, should we
choose to cultivate humanity through the: **"MASTER'S PLAN."**
KBA

"The reason why the world lacks unity, and lies broken
and in heaps, is because man is disunited with himself."

Ralph Waldo Emerson

My last night in that dorm, we filed out for chow in the evening, and I noticed that a young Latino man that had been assigned to the cell next to ours' ran out of his cell when that cell door popped open, he really looked distressed! He filed downstairs with the rest of us, yet he kept looking back at the cell he had just exited. We filed out and made our way to the chow hall. I kept my eye on this young Latino kid, he couldn't be no more than twenty, he looked very uncomfortable, and he wouldn't eat, he gave his food away. After chow, just before we entered the dorm, I watched that same young man step out of line and ask to speak with an officer.

We continued to file in, and as soon as we were all in our cells, three officers ran upstairs to the cell that young man had been housed in, pulled his cellmate out at gunpoint, laid him down and handcuffed him. One officer remained at the entrance to the cell until the crime lab personnel arrived. They went in with full Tyvek suits on, gloves and dust masks. You could see the flash of pictures being taken, and then the cleanup crew was called in, **inmates** in Tyvek suits, dust masks and gloves too. They began to drag all of the bloody sheets and blankets out of that cell.

That young man had been raped by the older Latino guy that had just been arrested. Chuck and I talked about this for some time. How sad and tragic it was that this scared youngster who had probably never been to prison before had been taken advantage of in such a gruesome way! And how the guy that perpetrated this grievous act is headed back to court with even more serious charges, **rape and sodomy**, which can carry a life sentence! What a precarious environment this is! The worse in society thrown in here with innocence and youth! Which equals **predators and prey!**

The next morning around ten in the morning, an announcement said Kenneth Akbar, roll it up, you're being reassigned to another dorm. I took a few minutes to thank Chuck for keeping it real with me, and I wished him the very best moving forward, then I gathered up my dirty linen, and meager possessions and exited that cell. I made my way downstairs, tossed that dirty linen in a bin and waited for further instructions. I was told to make my way directly across the prison yard to dorm one, where I would be assigned to another cell.

As that huge automated door opened to the outside yard, and the fresh outside air rushed in, I filled my lungs with it. I purposely walked around the long way so I could observe all of the activity on the yard. Men in prison blues and in orange jumpsuits were going to and fro. Some were walking the track that encircled the yard, and others were congregated off in their own segregated groups. Some were on the basketball court playing basketball and some were on the weight pile working out. All of the buildings had large numbers on them and there were four different buildings on this yard.

I noticed that some of the men in prison blues had their shirts and pants creased and boots polished military style. These men went in and out of the first three buildings almost at will, and they had a swagger about them like they were special or had special privileges. As I walked past some of these men they greeted me, and a few of them asked if I was endorsed to stay here at Tehachapi, and if I knew where I would be working. As I got closer to building one, I noticed men entering and exiting this building, greeting each other in passing.

There was a huge cylindrical tower that had to be fifty or sixty feet tall, the top of it was all glass, providing the officers in it with a panoramic view of the yard, and a gun port was open with the barrel of a rifle protruding out of it. As I approached the entrance to building one, there were a few guys already standing at it, awaiting the officer to pop it open. I stood there in silent contemplation, pondering what experiences awaited me in this one, and I prayed silently to **GOD**, whatever they are, that **HE** guide my thoughts and actions daily, and that **HE** keep **HIS** protective grace around me as I entered into this next phase of my sojourn.

> "And whatever of comfort you have, it is from **ALLAH**. Then when adversity touches you; to **HIM** you cry for help."
>
> QURAN 16:5

CHAPTER 6

"PIA AND PWC'S"

"Don't make your mind your prisons."

WILLIAM SHAKESPEARE·

I WAS ASSIGNED to cell 152, on the upper tier, in dorm number one. I didn't realize upon entering this cell that this is where I would do the rest of my term here at Tehachapi, in this cell. Upon entering the dorm I noticed there was an entirely different type of vibe in here. **Inmates** were seated at the various metal tables bolted to the floor in civilian attire. New sneakers like those on the streets, very nice sweat suits, and jogging suits; playing card games, drawing, playing chess or checkers.

    Some were turned around facing the nice color television sets bolted up high against the walls, and some were on the telephone or congregated in groups off to themselves. I got a lot of "what's up's and nod's from the brothers as I entered the dorm. I made my way up the stairs to my tier, and the officer popped open the cell door. Upon entering this cell, I noticed immediately that I had no cellmate! There were no tangible evidences of anyone being in this cell, and both mattresses were rolled up, which meant: **GOD** is so amazing! **HE** will grant you the desires of your heart!

I needed to be alone for a while anyway, as I begin to analyze this new environment I've been placed in. It also means that I'm not playing the radio with anyone that comes to join me in this setting! I stopped right then, washed up, and fell to my knees and asked **GOD** to bless this concrete cubicle; to make it not my prison, but my incubator, my cocoon, from which I shall return to and spring forth from, even in this environment, with **YOUR WILL** on my heart, not mine! Use me **LORD**, especially in here, where your children have wandered to such depths of darkness...

> "Darkness cannot drive out darkness, only light can do that. Hate cannot drive out hate; only love can do that."
>
> REVEREND DR. MARTIN LUTHER KING JR.

> "YOUR word is a lamp for my feet; a light on my path."
>
> PSALMS 19: 105

"IF YOU DARE"

I'm not playing, I am definitely going somewhere, and I
do trust and know that my **LORD** will see me there.
And as I feel my destiny drawing near, I will approach it
very head strong, with nothing but my **LORD** to fear!
There are those that have said, you're ahead of your time,
all I see is this mountain, and much more to climb!
So I cannot afford to carry any unnecessary dead weight,
I'm already behind schedule, I'm running way too late!

> The very top of that mountain is what I do truly seek,
> an overview of humanity from the mountain's peak!
> Much broader than man's world of chance and circum-
> stance, to that type of music, I no longer wish to dance!
> The invitation is still open if you wish to go there; **WARNING**,
> this journey requires discipline**: "IF YOU DARE!"**
> KBA

So I wiped down the metal bunks, I managed to get some cleaning products from one of the officers. I wiped down the entire door, inside and outside, I wiped down the one metal bookshelf bolted to the wall. I used an old T-shirt to wipe down everything with ammonia. Then I took ammonia and water and wiped down the entire floor, even under the bottom bunk, I managed to slide underneath to be able to reach the floor, and wall it was bolted to. Then and only then, did I make up my bunk. The privileges here were really different, you could go in and out of your cell as many times as you wanted to, I watched the *inmates* of every ethnicity go back and forth freely. Several *inmates*, from different interest groups and factions, were watching me as I went about my own affairs, *I felt it.*

As soon I thought this, the *charade* began, different brothers began approaching my cell door, asking me if I am affiliated; gang affiliated that is; what's my name; and each wanted to now give me their own perspective about what prison is, and has been for many of them for years! I listened to each of them and said: I'm a *Muslim,* nothing else. No lengthy explanations, no justifications, no reservations, nothing. I didn't come to prison to make friends with anyone! That was my motto, and I lived by it!

A few hours later, I had some very distinguished young men approach my cell door and say: *As-salaamu-alaikum my brother, while peering into my cell door with a smile as if they knew who I was and certainly knew WHO sent me!* One of the Muslim brothers that was persistent, was **Manteen**. He came to my cell door, and asked if I would join him and other Muslims at a table downstairs. I asked how do get the officer to let me out of this cell? He said grab a piece of cardboard or even a sheet of paper, slide it through the crack in the door and wave it, and I did. The door popped open and I stepped out of my cell and joined the brothers downstairs.

We had an interesting conversation. I introduced myself to everyone, and gave them some background information about me. Manteen had come down from level four, he had already served four years on a fifteen year sentence. Manteen noticed that I did not have a cellmate, so he asked if I would consider allowing him to become my cellmate. I told him I would consider that, and on that note, I gave my salutations to the brothers and returned to my cell. The next morning, the cell doors popped open for us to go to chow, breakfast, unescorted, to the chow hall. After breakfast, we returned to the dorm, and an hour later, the doors popped open again for work assignments.

I had to go to the administrative offices to have my picture taken, and I was issued my photo identification. I remained on the yard for a while, walking the track around the yard for some early morning exercise. I returned to the dorm right before lunch, washed up and fell to my knees in prayer. It is now February up here in these mountains, and it is starting to get really cold and wet. Snowing from time to time. Later that evening, I was informed by one of the officers that I must report to the **Prison Industry Authority**, the factory tomorrow morning. I returned to my cell and stood at the door upon closing it, just looking at the routine of things in this prison dorm, it was so predictable.

Some of the same comforts and conveniences of free society are afforded here. *Inmates* are allowed to receive packages from love ones and family on the streets, which can include can goods, books, certain sneakers, sweat suits, packaged pastries, CD players and CD's, etc.. There was also prison catalogs from which items could be ordered directly, and there was the canteen store on the prison yard, where staples, can goods, pastries, top ramen, rice, and other things could be purchased, even vitamins and protein powder.

Many of the *inmates* had television sets sent in by love ones so they could watch TV in the comfort and security of their prison cells. I made a pact with myself right then, that I would not have a TV or CD player sent in here for me, only books, clothing and staples. I watched each day as these men lined up in the day room to receive games from the *man*, chess, checkers, decks of cards, and dominoes. They would sit down in the day room and play their games, often gambling under the table, and often trash talking or boasting about all of the evil that brought them to prison in the first place. I made a point to stay away from all games while serving my time. Many fights, or arguments that led to fights, began over these pastimes or the prison telephone.

The next morning, I prayed fervently, and after breakfast, I steadied myself for the next adventure, the *P. I. A.* In addition to the information Chuck had shared with me, other *inmates* in this dorm had also corroborated these horror stories about this factory. So I prepared myself mentally and emotionally for this next challenge in my prison experience. The doors popped open and off we went, all of us headed out the dorm to some type of work detail. As I approached the entrance to the factory, I noticed that metal detectors and officers were there to 'check us in and out. I walked over, handed the officer my ID, and stood to the side as other *inmates* walked pass me to their work assignments.

In a few minutes, a burly looking civilian prison person walked over and gestured for me to follow him without opening his mouth. I followed him as he took me to a work station, laid pieces of sandpaper on the table, and explained that I must sand chair frames as they come out of the planer. I have to do this at a pace that does not interfere with the assembly line fluidity. Other *inmates* were waiting on these parts for assembly further down the line. I noticed that none of the other *inmates* had gloves, so I didn't embarrass myself by asking for any. The burly prison staff that escorted me into this place, whose name I found out later was Jack, was the *overseer* on this *plantation.* He walked up and down this assembly line barking derogatories and expletives at all of us during the day.

He would get right up in our face, and say things like this: **What's your problem boy? You ought to have a lot of energy cause you aint got no hoes to run up in, in here boy!** If you looked at him askance, he would taunt you by saying: **You got a problem with me boy? If you so much as look at me like that again, I will hit this buzzer on my side and have five cops on your head with their Billie clubs so fast you won't even know what hit you! So turn your ass around and put your focus on that dam wood!**

> "Vile deeds like poison weeds bloom well in prison air, it is only what is good in man that wastes and withers there."
>
> OSCAR WILDE

At the end of that degrading experience, my fingertips were burning and wreathing with pain, from sanding against that hard wood without gloves! I returned to the dorm, showered, prayed, and decided to take a nap. I was awakened an hour later by a knock on the cell door, it was an officer, I raised up and he said: You have a package, you need to come down to the office and get a pass to go pick it up. *A package?* Ok... I got dressed, flagged the tower to let me out, got my pass and proceeded across the yard to pick up my package. I was handed a medium sized box and I returned to my cell with it. When I opened that box and saw all the items that Terri had put together for me in this box, new sneakers, sweat suit, long johns, thick socks, some books, writing paper, envelopes, pens and pencils, can goods, and a beautiful journal. She also placed a beautiful greeting card with so many colorful expressions of love to me in it! **Man, I miss that woman!** In the card was also a phone number and time to call so I can finally speak to her! Yeah! I washed up immediately and fell to my knees, thanking my **LORD,** fervently for all of **HIS mercies and grace,** especially now more than ever!

The next day after work and chow, I made my first entry in my new journal:

02-27-96............ 6:30pm............ "All praises are due to GOD," It's snowing up here in these mountains this morning. I began my day with prayer, then off we go to the PIA, (Prison

Industry Authority), for some slave treatment and wages. "GOD is the greatest!" I received my first package, containing this journal. This is my first entry. I will need to recapture some moments on paper in here; my initial orientation to the California Department of Corrections, to where I am this date. Believe me, this is the stuff that makes Best Seller novels and Block Buster movies! The Zulu was rather tired, retired to the bunk around 8:30pm....

It's Friday, and Manteen reminded me to join him and other Muslims in the Chapel for Jumah prayer. He informed me that the authorities in the P.I.A. will be required to release me to attend the Jumah prayer. So this was definitely a Good Friday! I was born in a very orthodox Judea-Christian household, and my father was definitely an Old Testament type man. *"An eye for an eye, and a tooth for a tooth," "Spare the rod, spoil the child."* Raised in the Church my Grandfather help found, American Methodist Episcopal Church called St. Paul, well within walking distance of where we were all raised in a community called Joyland. When I was a kid, our community life, schools and Church was so much a major part of our lives.

We were always at Church! I was born in 1958, in the South, so I grew up in schools before **Desegregation.** I have vivid memories of these very proud African American educators before desegregation; our schools were all Black, and all the staff seemed more like family than educators. Teachers back then would exact corporal punishment toward students when necessary with a wooden paddle or leather strap. And in our communities at that time there was so much pride in the families. The old African proverb: ***"It takes a village to raise a child,"*** was a prominent theme of our community life! If you misbehaved on the far side of our community, blocks away from home and an adult saw you, you would get reprimanded there and then they would call or escort you home to your parents.

If you got reprimanded at school you knew you were subject to greater reprimands when the school or teacher contacted your parents. Although I was raised in the Church, I had issue early on with some of the blatant contradictions I saw. The facts I found myself confronted with as a child in the South, did not match the viable solutions offered by the Church, (to me), for the ills African Americans faced every day in the real world. Then in my Church, right behind the pulpit and choir, was this huge, beautiful glass stained image of **JESUS CHRIST.** The problem with that is, this **JESUS** was a pale, blue eyed Caucasian with long, stringy blonde hair! And the "Old English" text of the Bible, (King James Version), the language of it made no sense to my peers and me. *I do realize today that these nuances had nothing to do with the true message of the Gospel, and the universal message of JESUS CHRIST!*

I grew up right at the end of Jim Crow laws; I was old enough to remember all of the violence and assassinations, wars, and political unrest of the sixties and seventies. I studied Topography and Geography, and became enthralled in History because there were major concerns regarding what I was being taught at home and in school. Like how could Christopher Columbus discover a land already inhabited for thousands of years? How in the world could **JESUS** possibly have had that type of pale, white skin in a region where it is one hundred and ten degrees in the shade? Why was someone going to such great lengths to **whitewash** history this way?

Why are all the images I saw of Santa Claus as a kid fat white men? When I learned that my father and mother went in debt to provide all of us with fantastic Christmas', I became incensed! I grew up in a very large family full of high academic achievers and educators, and none of them could answer these troubling questions or chose not to. *I would get in trouble at school and at home for asking too many dam questions*! As I approached adolescence, I began to rebel against the lies and any institutions that promoted them, which included my father's leadership.

As a kid and a teenager, Muhammad Ali and Bruce Lee were my two heroes! I became interested in Islam following Muhammad Ali around the world in the media and magazines. I even got to meet Muhammad Ali in person when he came to Atlanta, where he put on a fundraising exhibition boxing match with then Mayor Maynard Jackson at the old Lakewood Fairgrounds. I studied the teachings of Elijah Muhammad, and later his son, Wallace D. Muhammad. Islam brought discipline and guidance back to my life that I lost in rebellion with my father, and taught me the significance of having a personable relationship with **GOD**. I changed my name legally from Kenneth Darryl Beavers, to Kenneth Bilal Akbar in 1979, and Annette changed her name to Rasheedah Aliyah.

So I gave Jack a slip from the office in my dorm that said I should be released before lunch to attend the Jumah prayer. *He looked at it, looked at me and said: I knew there was something weird about you, one of them dam Muslims! Go over there and get your ass to work!* So I did, and those few hours seemed to fly by. *I was released to attend the Jumah prayer, where I encountered a very distinguished, older man who was the Imam Yusuf Islam, the Chaplain for Muslims. He gave a most eloquent sermon, appropriate for those of us in the "Belly of the Beast", and reminded all of us that we are in here for disobedience before GOD, just like Jonah.*

> "None has the right to be worshipped but you oh *GOD*, glorified are you and truly I have been one of the wrongdoers!"
>
> QUR'AN 21:87

> "And just like Jonah, we can redeem ourselves if we return to strict and unconditional obedience to *GOD*"
>
> IMAM YUSUF ISLAM

> "From inside the fish Jonah prayed to the **LORD** his *GOD*. He said: In my distress I called to the **LORD**, and **HE** answered me. From deep in the realm of the dead I called for help, and **YOU** listened to my cry."
>
> 2 JONAH 2: 1&2

After Jumah, we all were required to return to our dorms for *fog recall*. This time of year up here in these mountains, fog descends down upon this prison like a thick blanket, you can't see your hand in front of you. So they lock us down, come around and do a head count to make sure none of us have escaped. We remained in our cells for several hours, during which time I did some reading. When the fog lifted, the officers popped the cell doors for day room, and Manteen came upstairs to my cell and said he needed to speak with me.

So I came downstairs and sat at a table with him. He told me he is clerk in the administrative office with the Lieutenant and Captain, and he also told me he heard them mention that a job as a clerk is open in Testing, and if I am interested, he would speak to them on my behalf. I said, **Allah-u-Akbar, (GOD is the greatest**)! Certainly I'm interested! Thank you for letting me know. I also told Manteen that he should let the officers know he would like to become my cellmate before they put someone else in there with me. He also asked if I would pray with him and other Muslims later in the dorm, and I said yes, I would.

I returned to my cell, washed up and prayed, thanking the **LORD** for delivering me from the clutches of the P.I.A. A few days later, I went over and met with the civilian prison staff in Testing, his name was Bruce. I will be assisting him with testing by passing out the pencils, answer sheets, and test booklets to new arrivals to this reception center. I will also be required to assist with grading the tests. I enjoyed the liberties in this new role, and I enjoyed it most because I got to greet all of the brothers, right off the bus. I became a liaison between brothers on the yard, and their home boys or family members that have just arrived.

A troubling trend that I saw, a trend in direct contrast to the law, is inmates whose tests I had graded, that scored well below acceptable literacy levels, were not sent to school or placed in a G. E. D. program because none existed at Tehachapi! To the contrary, I saw many that had been endorsed to stay here in the P.I.A.! I mentioned this fact to Bruce in Testing and he said: Well, nothing to do about that, it's out of my hands and beyond my reach to address. I went to the library and embarked on some study. I wanted to find out about literacy rates. I wondered how many of these men in here, are in fact, illiterate?

What I came across a few days later almost knocked my boots off! ***Sixty-five percent of all men and women that end up in prison are functionally illiterate!*** Wow! Wow! I returned to my cell and began to draft a letter I would ask Manteen to drop off to the Lieutenant, with a cc: for the Captain about illiteracy in prisons, and see if we can create a G. E. D. program so these men can return to society better off than they were when they came in. As I sat there looking at the snow falling down outside through my window, a surge of inspiration came over me, and this poem was born:

"IF YOU DIDN'T KNOW"…..

"IF YOU DIDN'T KNOW"

What compelling thoughts I feel, they encapsulate me, as I gaze
out at these snowcapped mountains up here in Tehachapi.
Subdued in silent contemplation, this experience isn't new,
the opulent inspiration of a poet, a very powerful overview!
A torrent imagination that's whipped into concrete form; abstract, enigmatic, and rutilant, outside of these social norms!
Unsullied by the degradation that this environment creates; corruption and hypocrisy just continues to permeate!
Just superficial efforts to offer rehabilitation to these men,
even in here the fiendish hands of capitalists is at the end!
Inmates endorsed to these facilities for their labor, called P.W.C.'s, kept ignorant and docile like medieval serfs; **no G. E. D.'s!**

> Multi-million dollar grants from the Feds, and major tax breaks, to cities that build these modern dungeons; what's at stake? An economic system that's rooted in perpetual evil, and your recidivism, I will probably be persecuted for promoting schisms! Yet I stand undaunted and intrepid in the face of the meanest foe; knowledge is only feared by tyrants and oppressors:
> **"IF YOU DIDN'T KNOW!"**
> KBA

I completed the letter, washed up and got down on my knees and thanked **GOD** for this gift and so many others, and asked **HIM** to please keep a protective hedge of grace and mercy around my family in my absence. I decided to go out in the dayroom for a change, too cold outside to go to the yard. I like to sit alone with a good book, or writing materials and pens for drafting a letter to my folks. As I sat there, I perused that entire day room, taking it all in. The Latinos and their various clicks off just to my right; Mexicans known as Pisa's, and their various clicks off to my left; affiliated African-American gang members and their various clicks directly across from me.

Skinheads and the Aryan brotherhood right behind me. All of them, off to themselves, lost in the philosophies and ideologies that bond them! As I sat there, a young man came in the dorm with a package his family or someone that loves him had sent him. He was smiling from ear to ear as he made his way to the far side of the upper tier. When the officer popped his cell door open for him to enter, he went inside and left the door ajar; I suspect with the intent of coming right back out. Then, four Black gang members walked up on the tier from different stairs, like sharks circling from different angles before the first, vicious attack!

I watched as one of them entered that young man's cell, then another, then another. In five minutes or less, they all ran out of that young man's cell with different items up under their clothing. The young man shut his cell door and stood there in the doorway for a while, in terror and disgust that his personal items had been lit upon by these **unrepentant thugs**! I found myself incensed by it! I used it as fuel for my workouts and training, for I believe someday soon, these and other atrocities must be addressed and put to rest. Manteen joined me later at the table.

He told me he should be moving in with me in a few days, the paperwork has already gone through for it. He also mentioned that there is a young brother named Jamal he would like me to meet later. The brother wants to make his declaration of faith to **ALLAH and Islam,** yet Manteen said he believes his decision is based more on protection than sincerity. Muslims in and out these prisons have always been known to demonstrate solidarity. The Muslim brothers in these places have been known for shutting down entire prison yards, **with just five devout Muslims too!**

Manteen told me had the hookup in the kitchen for fresh vegetables, fruits, and specialty sandwiches, cheeses and other items, so we will certainly eat well when he moves in with me. I went to chow that evening, had dinner and returned to my cell. Later that night my stomach start cramping, it got worse throughout the night! I began to vomit violently, and later diarrhea hit me. I was up and down all morning! I must have been food poisoned! Now with my immunity compromised, I got hit with the double whammy! A Flu virus going around the dorm came by to see me!

Now I have body aches, fever, head and chest congestion on top everything else! I was so sick I couldn't go to work or anywhere else for that matter! After a couple of days of all this, I had to go to the infirmary; go back and see that same quack I said I hoped never to see again! I went to see the doctor and he did prescribe some antibiotics for me. I stayed on my back a few more days before things began to improve. After this, I vowed to stay out of that chow hall as much as is possible, prepare my food in the cell rather than eat there. Manteen moved in a few days after I got better. He had a lot of stuff which included a TV, and books, a lot of books. Yeah! Later that evening, I went out into the day room with Manteen.

It was the first time I had come in contact with others since being sick. We sat down at a table and were joined by Jamal, the brother Manteen wanted me to meet. The brother made really nice, artistic greeting cards that he sold to others for stuff from the Canteen. We sat and chatted for a while; he said he was from Riverside, and a number of his homeboys were here in the dorm with us. They already objected to him affiliating himself with Muslims, and a few of them walked pass our table to snarl at him. As we sat there, one of us his gang affiliated homeboys named Smoke, walked by and snatched away some of his card stock that he used to make his cards with!

So Jamal jumped up and went after him. Manteen soon followed, and so did I! Smoke told Jamal in front of us that he was just playing with him, but since you brought your new Muslim friends over here with you, I am not going to give the card stock back to you! Manteen explained that in our faith, if you take from one of us, it is as if you took from all of us! Manteen said return Jamal's card stock or this situation will be met with swift justice! Smoke said: oh yeah! Since you are the big mouth of your group, you and I can deal with this in my cell or yours tomorrow morning, and Jamal, you are going to face my Lil homie Street, tomorrow evening. Manteen said are you serious?!

Alright, tomorrow morning, top tier, my cell! I returned to the cell with Manteen, and soon as the cell door shut, he began strategizing with me about tomorrow's show down. He began to move books and any other property of his that could be knocked over in a scuffle. He said he would move the TV in the morning. He told me that once that fool comes into the cell, he wants me to step outside and shut the cell door behind me and let no one in! I agreed, even though I did have my own reservations. I've seen men get stiffer prison sentences than the one they are already serving behind stuff just like this! I washed up, performed the wudu, and made salat with Manteen. I read myself to sleep, and awakened the next morning to Manteen stirring around early.

I sat up on my bunk and asked if everything was ok? He said yes, yet I knew Manteen was restless due to this looming physical confrontation. We made the wudu, and made salat together, then went to breakfast a while later. After we returned from breakfast, Manteen began to move the TV and any other items out of the way. I noticed that he put water in the electric kettle he brought with him and began to boil some water. As the water boiled, Manteen paced back and forth in that cell. When the door popped open for work detail, Manteen said this is it! Remember the instructions I gave you, let no one else in this cell but Smoke, then shut the door after he enters.

I said ok. I slid the door open, Smoke walked in, I shut the door and went downstairs where some of Smoke's homeboys were standing around. It seemed like all eternity yet I'm sure that only a couple of minutes had expired. I went back up on the tier near our cell and I could hear Smoke screaming under his breath. A minute later, Manteen said signal for the officer to pop open our cell, and I did. Smoke walked out of our cell holding his side and I walked in. Just as I walked in, Manteen walked out and said cleanup that mess up for me please, then he shut the cell door. I looked down and there was blood all around the sink, toilet and floor! There was an old T-shirt used for cleaning, I used that to cleanup as much of that blood as I could.

Fifteen minutes later, Manteen returned and cleaned up the rest. Later I asked Manteen what is it you did to Smoke that caused all that bleeding. **He told me that water you saw me boiling, that was for Smoke, as soon as he stepped into this cell, I hit him with that hot water, and then I shanked him**! He will think twice before he runs up in somebody else's cell! I'm sure he will! Later in the afternoon Manteen and I went out into the day room because now Jamal had to square off with Street in his cell. We had to make sure it was only those two, that it would be a fair fight. Jamal came to sit at our table and you could tell he was as nervous as Don Knotts!

He told Manteen he was just going to let them have the card stock, he would get some more. When Smoke and his henchmen came over, Jamal told them, you can have that stuff, it aint worth fighting over! Street said his homeboy Smoke got shanked behind your stupid card stock! You will fight me, or get stomped on for not fighting! Street walked over to Jamal's cell, signaled for the officer to open it, and when he did, he walked in and signaled for Jamal to join him. Jamal looked around at all of us and walked toward his cell reluctantly, stepped in, then turned around and shut the door with his back to his foe in that cell, **Big Mistake!** He disappeared in the blink of eye, and all you could here was the thudding of blows being levied against him! A few minutes later, Street walked out and shut the cell door behind him, then ran around the day room saying: *I made him shit all over himself*!

"MY PEOPLE"

My people, why do we fight and hurt one another? So
much envy and hatred toward our sisters and brothers.
My people, once Rulers of great civilizations, now we
are leaders in our own perpetual, self-annihilation!
My people, really distracted by this man's nation, many
of our minds are still lost on his modern plantations!
My people, will we ever regain our true form, which
does not have to lie in this man's westernized norms.
My people, may **GOD** continue to guard us while we
sleep; for we are the ones, the proverbial lost sheep.

KBA

"Violence is the last resort of the incompetent."

SALVOR HARDIN

"*ALLAH* is with those who restrain
themselves, and those who do good."

QURAN 16: 128

CHAPTER 7

"THE HYPOCRAZY"

THE YOUNG BROTHER Jamal tried his best to avoid coming in contact with the prison staff because if anyone of them happened to see all the knots and bruises he sustained in that beat down, he would be rolled up immediately, for his own safety, while they investigated what led to his injuries. One week later, an officer went to his cell door and told him to step out, when he saw what we already knew, he took him straight to the infirmary while another officer entered his cell. Right after that, the dorm went on lockdown. An investigative team of officers came in and entered Jamal's cell, pulled out his cellmate and questioned him outside while they searched the cell.

When this occurs, they will usually hit all the cells in this dorm, which means we will be on lockdown for a while! Many officers will descend upon this dorm, and one cell at a time, they will pull us out in our boxers only and turn these cells upside down for good measure! Personal items will get recklessly tossed around everywhere, and any contraband found will get you rolled up! Manteen knew the routine, so he encouraged me to gather my pictures, documents, and any other items I don't want destroyed and put them away in something sturdy! Thirty minutes later, our cell door popped open, we were told to step out and stand against the wall facing the gun tower, while they ransacked our cell!

Once they were done, we returned to our cell. It had been turned upside down, stuff thrown everywhere, they even stepped on our top ramen soups, cookies and other items. After spending an hour putting that cell back into some kind of order, Manteen and I did the wudu and performed the salat together before retiring for the night. The next morning, the announcement was made for breakfast, and thirty minutes later the cell door popped open for chow. After chow we all went out for work. Manteen returned to the cell later that afternoon and told me that his custody level had dropped lower, and he would probably be transferred to the two yard here at Tehachapi.

He asked me to consider stepping into a greater leadership role with the Muslims on the yard and I told him I would consider that. I asked him did he give the Lieutenant the letter I had drafted regarding the need to start a G. E. D. program here and he said that he did. Two weeks later, Manteen was reassigned to the two yard, and within a few days I received a new cellmate, Mike, he too was Muslim. A mild mannered laid back brother that had a certain peace about him. It is now March, and I made another entry in my journal:

> 03-16-96........ 12:15pm........ My **LORD** is **GOD SUPREME**, there is no **GOD** but **HIM**, **HE** and only **HE** could give me all the blessings **HE** has, now, and forever more! Because I have renewed my life and love for **HIM**! This has been another blessed week. I received mail from Terri, my love, my life, my wife, on Wednesday, 03-13-96.... It was the first time I had heard from her in over a month! Her letters, (three of them), really touched my heart! She expressed

*in each one, how much she loved me. The **LORD** really answered my prayers! **HE** kept her safe and secure, and in the word, **LORD**! Her last letter was from the reception yard in Fronterea, near Chino. May **GOD** continue to keep her safe, secure and blessed! I mailed a letter to her immediately!*

Today I embarked on a strict diet, high protein, low fat diet, eating more in my cell and less in the chow hall. I also began a very rigorous workout regimen, which included calisthenics, isometrics, and cardiovascular training, running outside on the track which encircles the yard regularly. I stayed out of the day room as much as possible. Most days now, when my cell door pops open for day room, I simply close it back. Then I would stand at the door for a while to observe the behaviors of all the men as they would spill out into the day room. It was so predictable, their behaviors.

Every day they lined up to receive games from the man! Decks of playing cards, dominoes, chess, checkers, even Monopoly! I watched from the security of my cell as they ran to the tables in the day room to get the best tables which also offered them vantage points where they could view the TVs while playing their games. There at these tables, they rehearsed and bragged about the very evils that brought them to prison! I thought to myself what is it I can do to challenge them to see what I see clearly every day. That there is no *correction* taking place here, which explains why the *recidivists' rates* are so high here in California.

The prison staff seemed to be really content with the way things are because this offers job security for all of them! ***So I committed myself on this day, to be an antagonist, an activist for reform regarding*** *the way things are being done. I began speaking with every officer I came in contact with, asking them about the State patch on their uniforms which said: California Department of Corrections and Rehabilitation.* I asked them; *what is being corrected with these men?* When the cell doors open for day room now, I also raced down to the office to talk to these men and the officers about these counter-productive pastimes of providing these grown men with games!

I also began to go to each table and speak with these men, asking them do they want to come back here after they get out, and all of them said no. I challenged them to see that if nothing changes while they are here, chances are they will be back! Many of these men had been coming back and forth to these prison environments for years! Some of these men had generational experiences with prison, their fathers and grandfathers had come back and forth to these dungeons for years too! I began sharing poems like this one I wrote many years ago, in the day room: *"HOW SOON WE FORGET."*

"HOW SOON WE FORGET"

How soon we forget: The repugnant
odor of our dead people's meat.
How soon we forget: The days we wore
chains on our hands and feet.
How soon we forget: Being placed on auction just like cattle and horses.
How soon we forget: Men in white sheets
and many screaming voices.
How soon we forget: The burning lashes of the master's leather whips.

> **How soon we forget**: Words of our hearts kept so far behind our lips.
> **How soon we forget:** Those that worked and died so that we might be.
> **How soon we forget:** The treachery of Slavery now that we are all free!"
> KBA

"Anytime anyone is enslaved, or in any way deprived of his liberties, if that person is a human being, as far as I am concerned he is justified to resort to whatever methods necessary to bring about his liberties again."

Malcolm X

I went around to the different factions of gangs and began to ask them, poll them about how they were introduced to gangs, and I began to ask them about their different gang philosophies. Then I asked them to look beneath the surface to see if it really makes any sense at all, that they shoot and kill each other over communities and streets that their families don't even own homes in or on. I saw that many of them had not even thought about the insanity of this generational, senseless bloodshed like this! So I compiled this poem to share with them: **"BRIEF"**...

"BRIEF"

Black faces…Strange places…Slavery traces…Very sad cases.
Broken homes…Daddies gone…Lonesome moans…On my own.
Tarnished streets…Gangs meet…Packing heat…Tagged feet…

> Mommas' crying...Sisters sighing...Defendants lying...People whying...
> No belief...No relief...Ageless grief....Life, so "**BRIEF!**"
> KBA

After a few weeks of challenging the men around me with these thought provoking poems and other relevant dialogue, when I stepped into the day room now, men would flock around me at my table to engage me about solutions and remedies to some of the problems in our communities and cities. This activity had made its way up the chain of command to the Lieutenant and Captain, so they began to make rare appearances in our dorm to see what this activity really was for themselves, and I seized the opportunity to go over and speak with them too, *about the ironies of prison life, and inquired about being granted permission to create a G. E. D. program for the men on this yard that really need that. They asked me what my angle really was. Am I trying to incite riots or disrespect for authority*?

I let them know absolutely not! I simply see what anyone one of them will see if they took the time to look at these men and their behaviors. They left the dorm without any further dialogue with me. Little did I know that they left instructions with the officers assigned to this dorm to step out and stand close by any area in the day room where I would conduct these talks. Some of the worse officers on the yard began to request this assignment. They would attempt to talk over me, or challenge me in front of the other men in this dorm about the irrelevance or futility of my efforts.

They nicknamed me Farrakhan, and tried to make humor of what they called my self-righteous talks. To discourage me from this, while I was in the day room, they would hit my cell, ransack it, and leave it that way for me to clean it up after day room was over. **None of their tactics worked!** I prayed and asked **GOD** for greater resolve and passion to do **HIS** will in here with these men, and to help me persevere through any harassment I could encounter as a result of it. I continued to go to the Lieutenant's office, asking about establishing a G. E. D. program on this yard. I also spoke with the Lieutenant and asked if I could be given the privilege of greeting the men in the reception dorm when they arrive here from County jails.

He said he would think about it. In the meantime, I aligned myself with some of the artist in our dorm that made greeting cards, and let them know I would partner with them. They would make the creative, colorful cards that they did, and I would do the poetry to go inside the cards for any occasion or event. After I did the first poem for one of the guys, I had others placing orders every week. I began sending greeting cards with my poems in them to my loves every week. I wanted and needed to be a source of inspiration to them, even in here. I sent this poem to my brother Tony, for all that he has done, and continues to do on behalf of family…*"I LOVE YOU BLACK MAN!"*

"I LOVE YOU BLACK MAN"

As I transfer these words from my heart to
this piece of paper for you Tony,
It doesn't take much deliberation to know
that you are the one and only.
Inseparable from the start; Atlanta; Tuskegee;
from the east to the west,
A brotherly love more durable than steel,
to this truth I will always attest!

> I could never thank you in words alone
> Tony, for all that you have done;
> In my aimless wanderings you never wavered; you looked after my sons!
> As I stare at this picture of you Tony, so debonair in front of that fireplace,
> I think of how much you mean to me, no time or condition can this erase!
> I'm so proud of you my Lil Big brother, continue on with your great quest,
> You're from the loins of Kings, and that's written in your face and chest!
> Please know that I walk out there with you, so be wise and understand,
> I'll turn Riverside into a ghost town over you,
> "I **"LOVE YOU BLACK MAN!"**
> KBA

I had a perfect card made for my sons, I had been informed by family and close friends that they were experiencing some challenges with each other, so I sat down and wrote this one for them: ***"AS I LOVE YOU!"***

"AS I LOVE YOU"
Will you remember?

That these words I have compiled for you are truth and no drama, verify this through any of your relatives, ask your Momma!

Will you remember?

When you were embryos, a small lump of undeveloped flesh, I made sure you were given the best nutrients, and nothing less!

Will you remember?

When you kicked and stretched inside your mother's womb, I talked to you and said: You will be out of there real soon.

Will you remember?

The day you entered this ole world I chose to be right there, I reassured your mother, and handled you with love and care.

Will you remember?

Right there in the delivery room, I gave you both your powerful names; I returned home and set up your beds before you came.

Will you remember?

I changed your diapers and handed you your
very first toy, I crawled with you, walked with
you, and you gave me so much joy!

Will you remember?

From a toddler to strong young men, I love you tremendously; that right now I pray for you daily, you mean the world to me!

Will you remember?

That your blood is my blood, if it is shed, mine
is shed too; that you should go out of the way
to love each other, **"AS I LOVE YOU!"**

KBA

My baby girl and only daughter, **Kenya Cierra**; I got to see her and her mother on a weekend family visit here at Tehachapi. She was seven then. . Although she was too young to really appreciate a poem from me like this, I sent her this one in a beautiful card: ***"HIS TEDDY BEAR!"***

Rasheedah and Ms. Kenya-age 5

"HIS TEDDY BEAR"

She brings me the greatest joy, although we have been apart,
my baby girl will always have a special place in my heart.
Three and a half years have gone by since I delighted in your smile,
or we laughed and played, or held you for a little while.
Many days and nights I prayed long and hard for your safety,
as I envisioned you with your mother, very clearly.
Look at what **GOD** has done, HE brought you
across country, on top of all that, **HE** sent
you to spend a weekend with me!
You see, **GOD'S HANDS** have always and continue to
guide us, and there is nothing we can't do if in **HIM**
we all trust.

> I had a lot of fun Ms. Kenya, when you and Mom
> visited me, it's true, and we had a chance to
> talk too, remember what I asked you.
> Stay faithful and pray; love and respect your mother; work hard at
> school, help at home and please mind your big brothers.
> Be strong, exercise, and no matter what, don't despair:
> your Daddy will be home soon to take
> great care of **"HIS TEDDY BEAR."**
> KBA

Today I met a dynamic brother, **New York**. He is originally from New York. This brother was well put together, even in here, and we talked more and more about how much we really did have common. Within weeks we were hanging out together, working out together, and jogging for hours together on the track outside. We challenged each other to get in the best shape of our lives while in here. New York was also a Muslim so we prayed together too. One afternoon when New York and I were sitting down talking in the day room, a young man new to the dorm came in with several bags from the canteen store.

Once he arrived at his cell door upstairs, and the officer popped open his cell door, *I saw the predators in the dorm on the move again!* I drew New York's attention to this and said those men are *cowards*, they prey on *scared young men* that are in here for the very first time, or *old men* that simply want to do their time and go home. They don't bother anyone! I was incensed! I told New York that something needs to be done about this! The way the prison staff have been dealing with this kind of stuff isn't working, too much stuff gets omitted! I'm tired of looking at this type of injustice right in front of me! That's when I really saw that New York's heart was just like mine!

Because his next reply was: ***What do you want to do about it? Whatever it is, I'm riding with you!*** I told New York, look, there is nothing we can do in this moment; let's put on our gear and go get a great run in and we will deal with it when we get back. He went to his cell and I went to mine to get dressed. As I looked over in the direction of that young man's cell I saw some of those **errant thugs** still around his cell feasting on a baby! I knew this would be one of my best runs, because I had some anxiety to burn off! It proved to be true! New York and I pushed each other like never before!

He outran me, then I caught up with him, and I outran him! This is a form of freedom that even some of these *free people* can't relate to or understand! Then we calmed down and got to pacing ourselves to run a good, hard steady pace! A pace that allowed us to have enough wind left to talk about what it is we planned to do upon re-entry to the dorm with these youngsters. I told him, just like always, when we go back in we will still be sweating.

We will take our gear off at one of the tables; because this time of year up here you still had to wear double layer clothing outside while jogging; then all I want you to do is wait at that table until I get back, Ok? I know you got my back, and I will never do anything to jeopardize our limited liberties in here, and our dates to be released. He said cool. We finished those last two laps like professional runners in a marathon! Even the officers in the gun tower on the yard had to tell us to calm down!

I guess they thought that we were about to run straight through the double perimeter gates. We walked a while for the calm down, then we stretched really good and made our way into the dorm. I purposely made my way to a table close to where those knuckle heads were. New York and I began to take our gear off like it was nothing, talking to each other while doing this. Once I pulled off the very last garment, exposing all of my upper torso, which was ripped up, like I was carved out of stone by now! I looked at New York and said: I will be right back. He said: cool.

I walked over to the table where they were all huddled up, sat down with them and before I could get one word out, several of those youngsters said: **Dam OG! Man you ripped the hell up! I aint never seen no man as yoked up like you!** I said thank you, then told all of them that the stunts I've seen you guys pulling with these youngsters in here, and the older Black men, it stops today!!! Because the very next time it happens, me, and my boy right there are going to run up in the cells where ever you are committing these offences right behind you, and shut the cell door behind you! **No escape!**

Then we are going to lay hands on everybody in there, except the victims! I explained to them that you get absolutely no respect by taking stuff from people that are already afraid of you! **Five of you against one man!** If you want some real stripes, come to my cell and take some of my stuff! **Understand?** Then I got up and walked back to the table where New York was, grabbed my gear and walked away with him. We talked about that encounter as we walked away, because we knew, in that moment, we put the fear of the **LORD** in their hearts, for some of them for the very first time, because they had gone so long unchallenged! **Guess what?** We never, ever had that problem in the dorm again!

"Few have the courage to bend history itself, but
each of us can have the courage to change a course
of events. It is from the numberless diverse acts of
courage and belief that human history is shaped.
Each man stands for an ideal, or acts to improve the
lots of others, or when he strikes against injustice, he
sends forth a ripple of hope, and crossing each other
from a million different centers of energy and daring,
those ripples build a current which can sweep down
the mightiest walls of oppression and tyranny."

BOBBY KENNEDY

"Verily! **ALLAH** loves those that are just."

QURAN 49:09

"And those who, when an oppressive wrong
is done to them, (they are not cowed down),
but help and defend themselves."

QURAN 42:39

A few weeks later, my cellmate was sent back to the County jail to address some other charges against him, so my cell was open once again. I let New York know this and the very next day he moved into my cell. New York, like I, was an advent reader, so we spent a lot time in the cell talking about the last compelling literature that we read. By this time, I had a sizable library in my cell, and

New York brought his own personal collection to the cell. In that concrete cell, we challenged each other to think outside of the box, and debated and deliberated over how we could make conditions better, if not for ourselves, for those that will surely follow us into these places.

We went around the prison yard and counted the number of young men in here compared to our age group and older. **The numbers were staggering! Six young men to every middle age man! So much displaced youth**! We decided to target these youngsters. A number of them had already asked if they could workout with us, so we began to encourage them to join us. In the day room, New York took one side of the day room and I took the other, talking to these men about returning to society stronger, wiser men. Before long, we had the respect and admiration of the entire dorm. Nothing went down in that dorm without our knowledge!

If there was a conflict between gang members or between anyone else for that matter, they came and got New York or myself to help mitigate it honorably. One day I got called to the Lieutenant's office, I got excited because I thought it was regarding the G. E. D. program we had requested permission to create. When I arrived in the Lieutenant's office he told me to come in, shut the door behind me and have a seat. His energy and expressions said this was not going to be an amenable encounter. He pulled out the Title 15, the standards manual for **inmates and parolees**, he thumbed through it and stopped on the page **regarding unauthorized congregating of inmates,** and then he turned the book around and placed it in front of me and said: **Read it!**

He said that with the authority bigger than his title and office! I read it, and when I was finished I turned the book back around and handed it to him. He said: ***With what my officers and I have already seen and documented we could put you and your cellie in the hole right now! I have no idea at all where you two guys think you are! This is a dam prison where individuals like you have been duly convicted of crimes, and therefore, remanded to the State for however long your sentence says; you guys belong to us, just like slaves!***

I squirmed in my seat while praying silently, then I told that Lieutenant that *slavery* was abolished in this country by President Abraham Lincoln, and it cost him his life! He looked at me and began to laugh so hard he nearly choked! When he stopped laughing, he leaned over his desk and said this where only he and I could hear it: ***Ok you educated nigga! You need to go back to school and learn some more! And I'm warning you Farrakhan, cease with the lectures in the day room and on the yard or I am going to make your life a living hell in here!*** I left his office steaming! I returned to my cell and immediately explained to New York what had just happened. So we washed up and made the salat, I remained on my knees for a while, imploring the **LORD** for **HIS** continued protection and guidance. When New York and I closed out our night with prayer, that experience and that fire inside me wouldn't allow me to rest, until this came out: **"ENEMIES AND ALLIES?"**

"ENEMIES AND ALLIES"

From the hulls of filthy slave ships to these dam prison walls, I see a legacy of pain and torture written in the faces of y'all!

Originators of prosperous cultures long before Greece and Rome, then nasty Western invaders infected   our utopian homes!
An institution of evil created by the Spaniards and Portuguese, designed solely for the Ashanti, Mandinka, Zulu, and Sudanese!
A diaspora like none other redistributed Africa's precious pearls, to the four corners of the earth, we built this man's new world!
Subjugated to subhuman conditions and far worse atrocities, rape, murder, and mayhem around us every day, listen to me please!
We were not released from slavery due to a change of heart, violent slave revolts and bloodshed, ready to tear this place apart!
Now addiction, immorality and deprivation is plaguing us in 1998. Have you ever thought about the origins of this sick self-hate?
Hundreds of years later and you and I still haven't realized; who am I? Who are you? Who are our true **"ENEMIES AND ALLIES?"**
KBA

"Finally, be strong in the *LORD* and *HIS* mighty power. Put on the full armor of *GOD,* so that you can take your stand against the devil's schemes. For our struggle is not against flesh and blood, but against the rulers, against the authorities, against the power of this dark world and against the spiritual forces of evil in the heavenly realms.

Therefore put on the full armor of *GOD,* so that when the day of evil comes, you may be able to stand your ground, and after you have done everything to stand. Stand firm then, with the belt of truth buckled around your waist, with the breastplate of righteousness in place."

Ephesians 6:10-14

CHAPTER 8

"THE STAND"

THE NEXT DAY, I couldn't wait to get to the library! I stopped in the Law library first, **to meet with the legal beagle of the yard: Mr. Ed Daire,** everyone went to him for legal advice and any paperwork, (appeals they had pending or any motions that needed to be filed), he was working on some stuff for me so I had a few minutes to sit down and chop it with him before reviewing the **language of the 13th Amendment of the Constitution.** That Lieutenant's laughter played itself over and over in my head. I walked around in that library until I found an encyclopedia, and in that book, I found it! As I read the language of the 13th Amendment, a numbness came over me, I was stuck!

"The Thirteenth Amendment, (Amendment XIII), to the United States Constitution abolished slavery and involuntary servitude, <u>except as punishment for a crime.</u> In Congress, it was passed by the Senate on April 8, 1864, and by the House on January 31, 1865. The Amendment was ratified by the required number of States on December 6, 1865."

I sat there, thinking about all the study and research I have done throughout school and at home, and I never remembered seeing that! I returned to my cell angry at myself, and this whole system! New York wasn't there, so I paced back and forth for a while, talking to my **LORD** as I did. **OH LORD, why out of all these men in here** *is it that I seem to be the one called to stand up against what appears to be years of oppression and ignorance? What is it YOU will have me do next? LORD, YOU already know so much and so many are depending on me coming out of here ok!* I sat down in complete silence, and *HE* answered me: *Why not you?*

Throughout history and in every generation, I have used people to help other people that are being oppressed and exploited. So right now, in here, I must use you, and be not afraid, because I AM always with you!

> "Indeed the mercy of **ALLAH** is (always)
> near those that do good."
>
> QURAN 7:56

I laid back on that bunk and closed my eyes, then I thought about a poem that I wrote to share with Nelson Mandela, when he was released from prison after all those years. There was a big event in Atlanta when he was released, he was flown into the city by the Mayor and other Dignitaries. The event was held at Georgia Tech's campus. All the local radio stations were there and you could call in and speak directly with Nelson Mandela. I called to share this poem and never got through: *"APARTHEID!"*

"APARTHEID"
Apartheid is taking peoples **GOD GIVEN** right to freedom,
we hear, and we see, yet our senses are numb.
We read it all in the papers, and see it all on the TV sets;
hasn't this blatant injustice touched us yet?

Do we ever wonder why these types of things happen? Or
are we just still too busy running and rapping?
African Americans should be doing all that we can, to elevate
the hearts and minds of our fellowman!
For we were once victims of the very same, this continual evil
which is only dressed up in a different name!
Apartheid is threatening the Humanity's right to exist, until each
and every one of us decide to emphatically insist!
That all of this insanity be brought to an immediate stop!
Absolutely no more bloodshed, not one single drop!
It is within all of our hands, yes we do all hold the key; Re-
member, Apartheid can only exist with our apathy!
KBA

"Dedicated to the legacy and memory of Nelson Mandela"

New York came into the cell and began to explain to me that he had been transferred to night shift for a while. Apparently there is a reshuffling of prison staff and inmates that is about to take place. He wasn't happy about having to work nights. I shared my findings with New York about the language of the 13th Amendment; he couldn't believe it either! We talked about other relevant issues like **Federal mandatory sentencing which gave birth to the Three Strikes Law in California.** Another clear example of why we must always be conscious in every moment!

Because if there was ever a time not to get convicted of multiple felonies in California, it was after 1994, when the Three Strikes Law was implemented! It took the discretionary authority Judges have always had since the earliest of times away from them! Even Kings had this power, to be able to evaluate each case on its own merits, and exact swift punishment or show compassion or mercy on a case by case basis. Now with mandatory sentencing, Judges now had to look at what the statue says regarding the punishment for that offense, and follow it strictly, which means any extenuating circumstances, or extraordinary variables can't be considered.

Which means, **First Offenders,** like the inordinate number of youngsters all around us up here, *that these hardened thugs see as prey,* is the outcome. I can't even name all the young men I came across right off the bus in Testing, that were **First Offenders** with sentences like forty years to life, seventy-five years to life, ninety-nine years to life; just laid over in reception before they head up to the **Big House, Supermax! Because Lifers** cannot be below level four security. I had to counsel many of these young men because they were terrified! I talked to them about controlling their fears, and I asked them if they believed in **GOD?**

Sometimes they asked me to deliver a message to a relative or homie on the yard or in our dorm. Sometimes I could sit in Testing with them after they were done; Bruce really didn't care as long as there were no issues. *They needed to confess their sins that brought them here to anyone that wouldn't use it against them.* Although the settings and characters were different, there was a familiar theme with many of them; little or no direction or leadership, **(broken homes),** so the streets full of drugs, alcohol, and gang violence seemed appealing! And many of these young men left babies on the streets to be raised by others!

So where does this carousel stop? Young women now looking for other men that are **ballers** to help them with these babies while procreating with these men from the same communities, doing the very same things which will inevitably lead them to the grave or these prison walls. And it just goes around and around and around! ***Perpetually! Self-propelled now by generational momentum!*** It's common to see women in our communities now with four or more different **Baby Daddies!** Yet when we really think about it, there should be no mystery why the family is so viciously under attack! The family is the incubator of the child, not just in the womb of women, but in the family for many years after the baby is born. There are many years of nurturing and protection that must take place in order for the child to grow unthreatened.

If our enemies can corrupt and contaminate the family, then our communities can be easily infiltrated and exploited! Our communities have been a rich resource for so many for far too long! During my earliest childhood memories, I remember when our communities were full of African American Educators, Artisans, and Business owners. Then the Five and Dime stores, Doctors and Dentists offices, restaurants, were taken over by other ethnicities. ***Why? What happened?*** Now it seems that even new immigrants that come to this country know in order to get rich fast, open Seven Elevens or Louisiana Chickens or 99 cents stores in our communities, ***because our people are no longer producers but consumers!***

Why is it in this country that when anyone of us begins a rally cry for solidarity and unity, and self-preservation, we get labeled as ***radicals or communists, or socialists?*** When it's apparent to anyone that's ***conscious,*** we can see clearly how well every other race looks after themselves and their own, quite well! What is it that veiled us to this fundamental need to look after ourselves? Could it be that after hundreds of years of slavery where some of the same corporations that exist today made fortunes untold off of torture, rape, murder, and mayhem; and after that, Jim Crow Laws, Disenfranchisement, the KKK and Lynchings, and the assassinations of every leader that came to improve the horrible lot of our people has had some effect on us? **You dam right it has**!

 I thought about some of the historic examples also, on the African continent and in this country. How the rank and file of great leaders and powerful organizations got infiltrated by our own people too, or let me say by people with the same hue and pigmentation as the rest of us. From Hannibal's military conquests in Europe; Chaka Zulu's reign in Africa; Rev. Dr. Martin Luther King Jr.'s efforts in Civil and Human Rights; The disintegration of the Black Panthers, and so on… I know for a fact that there are stooges in our dorm that have been planted there to give daily accounts to the man regarding our activities too! *So for all of them I dedicate this poem written many years ago just for them*: "SLAVE TRAIT!"

"SLAVE TRAIT"

You come into the house from out in the fields, before master Earl you passively kneel.

You begin divulging all the latest news, about your
sisters/brothers perspectives and views.

Selling your own manhood for a meager price, and
the future of your people is the sacrifice!

You kneel before a man as if he is your **GOD,**
then while in the Church all you do is nod.

> You sit around and boast because they don't yet,
> but when they do you will definitely regret!
>
> That you sold them out, you took the master's
> bait, you are less than a man just an ugly
> **"SLAVE TRAIT!"**
> KBA

New York and I went on for hours! Then he started to get dressed for his first shift on nights. Before exiting the cell we greeted each other and I said good night. I prepared myself for bed, made my salat, and went off to sleep. The next morning I awakened early around five, I washed up and prayed. While on my knees, a voice spoke clearly to me, and said: If you want **ME** to look after your children out there on the streets, you had better do all you can to look after these young men in here! By now, I had already missed both my sons High school graduations. My oldest son Mikal was already in Junior college playing football as a wide receiver, and Hakim had accepted a full scholarship to play football at the University of Washington. Hakim was an All-American Strong Safety in High school, and was being recruited by a number of Division 1 Colleges. Two recruiters had even come into the prison to visit with me, to offer not only Hakim, but the whole family all kinds of perks if Hakim was to choose their school. Hakim tried to get me to choose the school with him. I refused to do that, I explained to him some of the important factors he should look for in a prospective school, which has nothing with the rest of us.

My brother Tony and both my sons came up here to visit with me during this time in the visiting room, so I had an opportunity to speak to the boys face to face about life choices, and I used my present situation as an example of how poor choices, or bad choices can have an adverse effect on your liberties and freedom. That fall, I got to see my son Hakim play football on National TV as a freshman, He started in the Secondary his freshman year! I wrote this poem for Hakim as a source of inspiration on the field; *"HAKIM THE HEADHUNTER!"*

"HAKIM THE HEADHUNTER"

With stats like a pro baller his High school senior year, he rushes the line ferociously, no size player does he fear!

Laying major hits is fun, to force a fumble a real treat; enjoying playing the game so much that he laughs in defeat!

Your running game is shut down, you decide to go deep; not! He is known for making receivers and tight ends weep!

The most accurate Quarterbacks have problems throwing his way; blazing speed and agility, he will make the play!

On Special teams he is awesome as he rushes in to block the Punter, He is number five with the Huskies, aka: **"HAKIM THE HEADHUNTER!"**
KBA

Once New York and other brothers found out that my son would be playing College football most Saturdays on TV, they secured the TV room so we could watch the games together. Although I know they do exist, *haters*, I had never run into so many men that chose the other team simply because my son played for Washington! They took bets amongst themselves in front of me that my son would get beat on a passing route or get run over by a running back! I simply smiled at them, for nothing could deprive me of the sheer joy I experienced watching my son play College football on the big stage!

> "You will face your greatest opposition when you are closest to your biggest miracles."
>
> SHANNON L. ALDER

We got to see a number of Washington's games on TV, one in which Hakim got an interception! Yeah! I began to spend more time in the Chapel, and whenever Imam Yusuf Islam was on the yard, I would go to his office to speak with him. I shared my personal history with him and told him about the ironies and hypocrisy that I and others faced here at Tehachapi. I told him about the written request that I submitted to the administrators regarding the need for a G. E. D. program for many of these men. He listened attentively, then he said he would use his office as Chaplain to support us in wholesome activities and programs.

He even told me that we could use the Chapel when available, so that we are not on the yard in plain sight of the officers when the need arises to speak with these men. I always left his office inspired and even more determined to use my time here at Tehachapi to help these men in whatever ways I could. New York was up for his annual review, and he already knew his custody level would drop, which means it's time for transfer to another facility. He and

I began to reminisce about all the things we had seen, discussed and addressed in the two years we had come to know each other and live together.

He had been a real **GOD SEND** to me and so many others on this yard, and now he would be sent to other places like this to help the men around him. I let the brothers on the yard and in our dorm know that New York would be leaving soon, so we all agreed to **throw a spread,** (we all would bring top ramen soups, can goods, vegetables and cheese; mix it all up and create a pretty incredible, eatable meal), for New York this weekend. We all got together and paid tribute to New York, thanking him for all he had done for so many. A week later, New York rolled up all his stuff, and he was gone. So now I am alone again in that cell, and I used that time to delve deep into study and prayer. *I studied the Torah, the Bible and the Quran.*

I noted all of the similarities in these monotheistic religions, then I thought about all of the denominational barriers that exist in these religions today. I studied world religions years ago in Atlanta, and I yearned to be used in a way that brought people together, not pushed them further apart. I remember the denominational arrogance in some Christian faiths from my childhood experiences, and thought about how today, all of the different warring sects of Muslims, when one of the primary definitions of Islam is peace. One day when I was engrossed in study in my cell, someone kept calling my name outside the cell, downstairs. I walked to the cell door and asked who is it? I looked through the glass and saw Ray Ray, one of the cool brothers I had known in the dorm for a while.

He said can you come out for few minutes? I've got someone I want you to meet. I said ok, and got dressed, then flagged the officer to let me out of the cell. As I walked down the stairs to the day room, I noticed Ray Ray was standing with a young man that had an athletic build and stern visage. As I approached Ray Ray, he said what's up Akbar? Then he said this is my young homeboy, **Foots**, he said he really wants to learn about Muslims and Islam, so I told him, let me take you to meet a real Muslim. I said really. So I shook the young man's hand and sat down at one of the tables to talk with him for a while. In that brief encounter, I began to realize just how much impact my efforts had on these me in here.

He told me his government name was Marcus, (nickname-Foots), and that he was born and raised in South Central Los Angeles, and he has been a reputed gang member since he was young. Then he told me that this is not the first time he had been in this type of environment; that he left behind on the streets this time, a wife and child, and an aging father that really needs him to get it right this time!

He explained that he had been exposed to Islam before and this time he wanted to delve in completely, and give his life and heart to **GOD.** So I told this young man that I would do all I can to help him. Every day after that, this young man would be waiting for me in the day room, to study and pray together. I gave Marcus the benefit of my insight and knowledge, and he loved it! I explained to him the demographics of this yard, and I shared with him the types of travails I and others like us have had to face because of what we stand for. By this time, at **GOD'S SPEED,** so many things had begun to change.

That racist Lieutenant had been reassigned to another prison and the Lieutenant that replaced him on the yard was more agreeable to programs and activities that promoted real rehabilitation in prison. I was granted the privilege of greeting the brothers in the reception dorm, to take their lunches to them, and offer them encouragement and insights about prison life, and Marcus joined me in this task. I also secured permission to use the Chapel to get brothers together; from different gangs and backgrounds during **Black History Month,** to talk about some of the historic issues and concerns in our communities, and to use poems like this one, as a rallying cry for change while in here: *"TIME IN VAIN!"*

"TIME IN VAIN"

There is no coincidence that we came together this
February, it was long overdue Black Man,
and I contend that it was necessary!
So that these words could be conveyed from me to you, eye to eye,
shock treatment to the head, and maybe later you'll ask why!
This Black History Month was established for all of us to reflect, on the
many examples that should increase our own self-respect!
It is time to shake those derogatories, don't believe
the hype, terminology like dog and nigga,
let's shake these awful stereotypes!
Each one of us is a King or Prince, yes so culturally rich, yet sinister
influences have us calling our women a trick and/or bitch!
Forty percent of our men in this sleeping nation are
inside these pens, our women and children
are now open for the enemy's den!
How long will this be our home away from home? Many CDC
numbers, viewing the world from TV in here, summer to summer!
How many of us take the time to study, or improve
our vocabulary? Lined up all day to get games
from the man, to the contrary!

Now that date is finally here so you are paroled to
the streets, daily pressures from society and parole for you and me to compete!
It's all about your paper huh? Getting your chips or getting paid,
until that Third Strike puts you away, or in the grave you're laid!
Another talented Black Man, gone from here
or totally emasculated, and the war rages on
while our families are being infiltrated!
My time has come to a close up here, and all I've tried to explain,
time used wisely wherever you are, is never **"TIME IN VAIN!"**
KBA

"We must use time as a tool, not as a crutch."

JOHN F. KENNEDY

Marcus and I embellished ourselves in **WWW.GOD, worshipping daily; working out rigorously, and working to make a better way.** He joined me on that boxer's regimen. I boxed for many years. The irony of that is I continued to train for many years after, and maintained a low fat, high protein diet. I raised my sons on that diet, and required them to workout with me by the age of ten. This consisted of long runs every other day, calisthenics and isometrics. The weight training came later. I had both my adult sons on **tiger milk bars and protein smoothies** when they ten and twelve.

So, praise **GOD,** we didn't have to invent anything new, just get down and dirty with the basics. Both Marcus and I were bulging through our shirts in no time! I knew my time would be winding down up here in these mountains. They told me in my last annual review that I should be eligible to transfer to a lower custody at my next review because I have not had any write ups. *I did a good program.*

In great shape on the yard at Tehachapi State Prison/1998

I smiled as I thought about my perception of what it meant to *program* early on in the County jail. My relationship grew with the young Marcus, it seemed like there wasn't enough day room time anymore. I told him that I would be leaving in eight months probably, and the only way that I can give him the time he demands of me, he will have to become my cellie. He said you would do that Akbar? That's cool. Let's roll with it! I put in the request with the officers in the dorm and the following week, he moved in. *A genuinely fertile and inquiring mind is one of the most amazing things to behold!* As Marcus entered that cell he was awed by the poster boards I had along the walls, with words like these:

"To Thine Self Be True!" *"Small minds speak of people, average minds of events, but great minds of ideas."* *"As man sees himself, so he is!"*, *"You owe it to yourself to always look on the brighter side of things." "The end of deeds begins in thought!"*

I had them written in dark bold print, and he couldn't stop commenting on them. I told him where he could place all of his belongings, then we talked for a while. He observed as I washed up in preparation for prayer, and followed it. Then I led us in the salat together. By the time we finished it was chow time so we got ready to go. The next day Marcus got his endorsement to work. That could always be a crap shoot! Is it the PIA? The kitchen? An outside yard detail? Or a clerk assignment. Well wouldn't you know it? Favor has smiled upon him because he is going to be a clerk in the Chapel. Poo Poo Pee Doo! (Smile).

Marcus went out to the yard for his job assignment, at this time he still had thick braids in his hair and walked with a swagger from the streets. He encountered a bigoted Sargent on day shift, with all his henchmen standing around with him, and they stopped the young brother. **Walking across that yard could resemble Apartheid South Africa!** You had better have your papers on you, and follow their commands or a physical, brutal beat down could be the consequence! He heeded their demands and even then they surrounded him like the cowards they are, Billie clubs in hand, snarling at the young brother, while yelling obscenities and expletives in his ears! Marcus was a lighter shade of brown, when he returned to that cell, he was red hot, and his nose was glowing!

I was seated at the table doing some reading. I sat back and allowed him to vent for a while, pacing back and forth in that cell as he did so! I suggested that he wash up, get the grime of the day, and that experience off of him. Then take it to the **STEADY HAND**, in prayer and meditation, and he did. When he rose from his knees, he approached me with a fire in both eyes and said to me: From now on Akbar, my name is *Mustafa Muhammad Shabazz*, henceforth, until it's finished legally! My brother, man! This is real spit! I'm changed forever! Words cannot express the joy of watching this young man come into his own new identity! No foe before me will ever make me waiver or stagger! Then that cock strong young man grabbed me and squeezed me with a tributary bear hug!

And we chanted: Sword sharpens sword! Wit sharpens wit! Let's go! There is nothing we can't overcome with **ALLAH, swt,** as our **FIRST FRIEND!** After that Zulu rally cry, the next day, I came back from breakfast with Mustafa, and he reminded me that he had a late show up time at work because the Chaplains don't have the normal schedule as regular prison staff. I said ok and left the cell for my day's adventure. When I returned to that cell after work, I returned to a young man that had made the transformation complete to himself! **He had shaved his braids off!** And seated calmly, he said to me: Ok Akbar, what's next? I know I need to make my declaration of Faith and Conviction before a believing Muslim and **GOD,** and I'm off on my own journey!

That's right young brother, and I'm honored to share this part of it with you! So he and I, in that moment and time, solidified a lifelong relationship that would transcend these prison walls in the most amazing ways, long after parole was discharged, and to this very day! I watched the young brother go at it on his own like a beast! We thanked **ALLAH**, *swt*, for the earthly vessel through which the world was blessed, and refurbished in the sixth century in the east, (Saudi Arabia), *Prophet Muhammad, sws*...Like has been the very theme of humanity from generation to generation, age to age, one epoch to another; ***struggle and progress.*** The best in man has always been and will always be based on **HIS DESIGNER'S** pecking orders, and not his own!

So Mustafa studied regularly after that, and though I loved to see the young man engrossed in study and ponder, there were times where I had to insist that we take a break, and go sweat one out on the yard, or I would challenge him to a dual on the basketball court, my second love after boxing. And I was really good at it, if I may say that modestly. Balance in all things is an essential ingredient to health and vitality. I saw the growth and maturity blossom in this brother in no time. We would have these intense debates in that cell about some of the most glaring concerns and issues that young African American males face on the streets in our communities and behind these prison walls.

And through this continuum, this platform ***T. E. A. was born! The Expiation Association. The word expiate means to atone for, to make amends, reparations…..*** For if all of us were to look at the conditions, circumstances that brought us in here, whether we violated the law out of ignorance or maliciously; even the courts position was and is, that we pay our debts and/or make amends to society and our victims by being deprived of our basic liberties and freedoms for a while, for the term of our prison sentences, and eventually upon parole if there are release dates, we should return to the society better off. ***In theory and principle of the law itself, this is true. The Huge Miscue is this: What these men do with their time while here, for however long, is the sole variable in real self-atonement, personal healing and growth.***

So Mustafa and I sat down in the succeeding days brainstorming on a complete charter for this organization. What is its mission statement? What supporting research and data is illustrated for its purpose and necessary existence? What tenets must its members understand, revere, and follow? We looked at historic, current, and even recent examples of major reform in this country and abroad through which a course of events effected the lots of people for the better.

One thing for sure that rang true from generation to generation, age to age is this: Whenever there has been suffrage and injustice in the world, those oppressed people cried out to their **LORD** for *deliverance* and a *deliverer* to guide them out of their horrible circumstance or condition. Raise up someone from amongst ourselves that will protect us, and lead us back to **YOU!**

> "He will deliver the needy who cry out, the
> afflicted who have no one to help."
>
> PSALMS 72: 12

Why is it that it should or must be someone from amongst themselves? Because who can best articulate those horrendous conditions before man and **GOD** except someone that has experienced it and sees it every day?

Like Moses, aws, for example. Although we appeal to and invite outside, positive influences to support us in this effort, **the work is ours to do**! For the sad and growing statistics in our African American communities all across this country in every category, such as teen pregnancies; High school dropout rates; rates of incarceration and murder for African American males ages eighteen to twenty-five are like no other race of people in this country; and rates of illiteracy are alarming! So there must be teams of insightfully trained personnel in our communities equipped with the tools and resources necessary to effectively address this!

Change like this historically has never come easy. There are individuals, corporations and even politicians that do not want to see any reform or change in this well-oiled machine called the CDC, and the private prisons that are springing up all over this country because of **unhappy shareholders. Capitalism at its worse!** So went spent the next few days researching and writing. Then we went out on the yard and in the dorm and introduced everyone to **T. E. A.,** and before long we had spiked interest in many brothers and conducted meetings in the Chapel. We sat around in a group setting, introduced ourselves to one another, and got the brothers to open up and become transparent about themselves, their families, and communities, and the thinking and behaviors that brought them here.

It really felt good watching these **hardened criminals**, drop their hardened facades, and be human again. Well Thanksgiving is approaching, and I have been informed that I will have the blessing of embracing my mother and other relatives again, because they are coming to see me after Thanksgiving. Yeah! Praise **GOD!** I miss my mother so much! I have had a very unique relationship with my mother since I was a kid. I was always in the kitchen when my mother was cooking as a kid, talking about I'm hungry. She had me help her with some things.

There were many benefits in doing that, I got to sample dishes; I learned their ingredients, and my Mom and I enjoyed each other's company while doing that. Our mother had multiple, major roles in our family. She did all of the shopping, all of the cooking, and all of the cleaning; we helped her with what we could, all of us were assigned chores as children, and were expected to perform them diligently. When I turned sixteen and got my driver's license, I drove my mother to stores and other places, I loved it! As I thought about my mother, and her mother, these two poems came to mind, poems that I wrote for my mother many years ago called **"SWEET LADY OF LOVE, and one for my mother's mother"** called **"BIG MOMMA!"**

"BIG MOMMA"

Big Momma how often I think of you, and all
the wonderful things you would do.
Big Momma impressions of you persist, embracing you none of us could even resist!
Your smile warms the coldest of hearts, as a grandmother you really played that part.
Your love like that of gentle wind, in you was
a grandmother and a genuine friend.
Big Momma I miss you so very much, your smile,
laughter, and especially your touch!
KBA

"Dedicated to the loving memory of **Inez Shropshire**"

"SWEET LADY OF LOVE"
"(MOMMA)"

As I ponder over many sources of love, very frequently it is you that I think of.

Your captivating, illuminating smile, the kind
that remains with you for a while.
The gentle touch of your warm embrace, that
sincere glow always on your face.
You held me near to you when I was small, you
helped me grow from short to tall.
You calmed my heart when I would weep, and
you guarded my soul as I would sleep.
You touched me in ways words can't express,
when I think of you, I know I'm blessed.
"SWEET LADY OF LOVE," I will never forget you, in my heart, your love is forever true!
KBA

"Dedicated to my mother, my Queen of Queens: **Gloria Shropshire Beavers**"

My mother's parents, **Inez Sims** and **Wayne Shropshire,** were from Palmetto, Georgia, a rural town about forty miles outside of Atlanta. Born during the Reconstruction era in this country when people raised their own chickens, hogs, and cattle and grew their own vegetables and fruits. I remember my mother telling me that they only ate meat on Sundays and that they lived off of a lot of beans, vegetables, cornbread and rice otherwise. **My mother, her only sibling Ruth and my grandmother had very light complexions.**

I was told this was because their great grandfather was a white man that raped their great grandmother. My grandfather lovingly known to all of us as **Big Daddy**, was the very first real gangster that I came to know. *As a matter of fact, the catalyst that brought my grandparents and their children to Atlanta was my grandfather* *drawing a pistol on two white men and pistol whipping them both because they thought my grandmother was a white woman, and they tried to assault him for being with her.* I spent a lot of time around my grandfather as a kid, he was a jack of all trades and an advent hunter and fisherman too, and he also gave me my first pistol when I was sixteen.

I thank **GOD** so much! For blessing me to be born in such a magnificent family! A family that has demonstrated throughout the years what unconditional love is, and certainly throughout all of my travails in life! A family that have traversed mountains and valleys to visit with me up here in these mountains! One of the variables I have seen with a significant number of the men here, is they don't have family, a solid support group of love ones to support them while here, and upon parole to the streets.

My oldest brother Artie, has been an excellent example of manhood and leadership for me since I was a little lad. He and my soldier Lil big brother, Tony, Kenya and Rasheedah came to visit with me. A month earlier, he turned fifty years young, (smile). I wrote this poem to honor him on his fiftieth birthday,*"FIVE-O!"*

"FIVE-O"

I reminisced about you and the fellows singing, and being jive, you were fifteen and I was only five.
The comradery I saw, I mimicked what you guys did and said, until June bug dropped me on my head!
That's the earliest age I remember you in the set, harmonizing the Duke of Earl; and blowing a trumpet!
As I began to mature, inquisitively wanting to know who I am, you got drafted and your way to Vietnam!
I do remember all of the letters and pictures you sent home, you in military fatigues in the war zone!

By way of **GOD'S GRACE** you were returned to all of
us at home, from a land far away, in the unknown!
Young, healthy, experienced and quite strong, deter-
mined now to start a lovely family of your very own!
A young family to support, you began a career in the Fire
Dept., every station you would leave your imprint!
From Firefighter, to FAO, to Lieutenant, Captain, now
Chief, an example of what can happen with true belief!
You took time to touch me and others, that's what
you're about, I'm indebted to you for Portsmouth!
So many other ways you have encouraged me in joy or
trial, I can't wait to see you, be home in a while!
This poem is sent on the wings of my love, so please
know, I'm elated to honor you, Happy **"FIVE-O!"**
KBA

From left to right: Me, Angela, Carmen Tia, Gloria and Reggie

Another historic entry in my journal:

"AL-HAMDULILLAH!"
12-15-98............Tuesday

Once again, I've been granted this excellent opportunity to record my thoughts and feelings in this historic journal. My concern and prayers are focused on Kenya and the boys right now. Please guard and guide us all during this time of transition and disparity, please watch over my children **LORD**! Mom, my sisters June and Debbie, my nieces Carmen Tia and Trisa, Tony and Hakim came to see me November 27th, the day after Thanksgiving. Man! They look so good! Praise **GOD**! Hakim has gotten so big! I felt like I was in the company of celebrities! I haven't seen Mikal in a while, I have talked to him though. He said he is headed to Washington now that Kenya and Rasheedah have gone back to Atlanta. One of my nephews that I had a direct hand in raising back home in Atlanta, **Johnathan**, known to us all as **Buck**, came out to Cali after graduating from High school to live with the boys, to train with them and to attend College out here. I'm elated that he has! Another year has come to a close. Next entry, **1999**!

From left to right: Me, June, Momma, Debbie and Tony

CHAPTER 9

"Transfer"

I KNOW MY time here at Tehachapi was drawing to a close. I spent more time preparing Mustafa to take on the roles of leadership for the men up here in my absence. The administrators finally gave consent for a G.E.D. study program. We had to provide the study manuals and work with the men in our own spare time and we did. What an appropriate closure to my time up in these mountains, to see something you have fought for over the past three years be finally granted, and your adversaries silenced about it! My last week in Tehachapi, all the men came out to thank me and honor me for the work I had done on behalf of us all. We had a big spread in the dorm, and afterwards, Mustafa called me out on the basketball court one last time.

All my personal property had already been packed away for transport, so I had to play him in those stiff prison boots. No excuses, he beat me pretty bad, and we laughed about how I slid across the court trying to guard him. A few days later, I was gone. California Mens Colony is located on the Central coast, and the bus ride up there was breathe taking! Beautiful coastline near Santa Barbara. Upon arrival, I was placed in the reception dorm, number eleven. Until you are completely evaluated, you must remain in the dorm, no yard time. It takes a week or so. I did not like the open dormitory type way these dorms were set up, rows and rows of bunks in an open dorm just like the military. No more cells! I was assigned to a bunk with a metal locker to house my things. After situating my stuff, I walked around the dorm, to get a feel for this new environment. Each race, (Whites, Latinos, and Blacks), had their own TV room. I stood at the back of the Black's TV room and noticed some of the same ignorance taking place, where gang members were flexing their muscles over the TV, refusing to allow anyone else to select programs except gang members, and arrogantly insisting that this is the way it is, and this is the way it will be! I shook my head and returned to my bunk! I pulled out some reading material and attempted to blot that image out of my mind.

Over the next few days, I noticed that this behavior continued in the TV room, now they were disrespecting older men that are simply trying to watch some of their TV programs. I went to the restroom, washed up and made prayer, making my peace with the **LORD!** Then I got up off my knees, grabbed the Quran and walked into the TV room. Five of these oppressors were still in the TV room, having run others off with their threats of violence. I walked in front of the TV, turned it off, and stood there in front of the TV and introduced myself to these men. I explained to them I am new to this prison, that I am a Muslim, and that I despise tyranny and oppression!

I put my hand on the Quran reverently, then I explained to them this is the Bible of Muslims and I live by it, and in this book, **GOD** says to us that if we die while defending the rights and liberties of the oppressed, we are guaranteed paradise! What you guys have been doing in this TV room with other men is scandalous and unjust, and it must stop today! For the very next time I see it taking place, I am going to go put on my boots and come in here to deal accordingly with anyone I see perpetrating these offenses! **Understand?** I walked out of that TV room and went back to my bunk. When the yard opened some of those guys went out and found Muslims that they have known on the yard for some time and explained to them what they encountered with some new Muslim named Akbar in the dorm. Once it was explained to these brothers, **brothers I had not even met yet**, what had actually happened, they were told if one hair on that man's head is harmed, you can expect swift retaliation from all the Muslims on the yard!

A new entry in the journal

"ALLAH-U-AKBAR"
02-26-99
Friday

Wow! What a difference a few days can make! Since my last entry, so many wonderful things have taken place. First of all, I have been blessed to experience a new year! My beautiful mother enjoyed another anniversary of her birth, 65 years of age, and she doesn't look nearly that age I had my evaluation and something amazing took place! Favor has found me even in here, because the prison staff initiated a request or interest that my custody be lowered for a special assignment to the Firehouse, **ALLAH-U-AKBAR!** Here I am on the Camp yard, a totally different environment to say the least! Today I saw this beautiful coastline on an outside work crew. Man! **The Pacific is so beautiful!** Its simple things like this that I took for granted a few years ago! A new chance, a new perspective about everything, that's where I am! I turned 41 a couple of weeks ago, I don't feel 41, whatever that means. Ms. Kenya will be 9 years old March 19th.

Upon being released from the reception dorm, I was assigned to the Two yard for a few months. Now I had the pleasure of meeting and interfacing with the Muslims that had stood up for this brother they had not met yet. **Brother Fareed, Malik, Yusuf, Ali, Rasheed, Jamal and so many others**. They welcomed me with open arms and asked if I needed anything at all. Later, we went to the Chapel, where *I was introduced to Imam Kamal Abdul Jabbar, the Chaplain for Muslims on the yard.* **He walked and carried himself in a way that demanded respect. He had a stern visage and immaculate appearance.**

The following Friday we attended the Jumah Prayer service where he delivered the Khutbah or sermon, eloquently and emphatically, *a sermon specifically centered to address all of us in here held captive by our own poor choices.* I worked out with the Muslims, prayed with them and broke bread with them, as they all began to explain to me some of the unique issues and concerns on this yard. I found out that this prison was an old Navy base that was active before World War II, and later it became an internment camp for Japanese Americans and other Asian Americans after the bombing of Pearl Harbor.

So now I understand why the dorms are set up like military barracks. This was a real adjustment for me and others that had grown accustomed to some sense of privacy in the cells. After a couple of months I was reassigned to the Three yard, which is the Fire Camp yard. **Inmates** on this yard will be trained thoroughly in wildland fire fighting techniques because we will be required to go out and assist the California Department of Forestry with fires all over the State of California. I was a Fireman in Atlanta for a number of years, so I had some formal training and experience already. My very first job assignment was that of a mechanic on the fleet yard, assisting with fleet maintenance of all the emergency vehicles, mobile kitchen and transport vehicles for the *inmates* being transported to these sites where forest fires were and/or to cut fire lines in areas where fires could occur. I enjoyed my role in this new job assignment.

The Fleet maintenance yard was off the prison grounds. So we had to be transported outside the prison gates to work. This area on the Central coast, in San Luis Obispo County, was a virtual nature reserve. Falcons, Hawks, Eagles and Vultures circled up high overhead; different species of snakes and lizards, and even rare frogs were all over the place. One day a few weeks later, I was on the fleet yard with other *inmates*, I heard a sound that resembled a loud motorcycle approaching from a distance.

When I looked in the direction that sound was coming from, I saw a black cloud approaching! It was an entire colony of bees, relocating the whole colony as they surrounded the Queen Bee! I yelled out to the guys, **Run**! We took off, and barely made it inside as this colony of bees swept pass us! I have been informed that when we must respond to these wildland fires, I won't be required to fight the fires. My job will be setting up and maintaining the Mobile Kitchen. A trailer had been converted into a mobile kitchen, fully equipped to feed *inmates* and free staff in close proximity to these wildland fires. This next entry in my journal best describes what I encountered in this role.

"ALLAH-U-AKBAR"
10-19-99   Monday

Well, months have passed since my last entry, and here I am being sort of despondent, huh? So many powerful events have come and gone. I have the distinction of being fire ready now. I've been to numerous wildland fires all across this great State! Slept outdoors on cots and sleeping bags, cracked from sun up to sundown while feeding thousands of fatigued firefighters. That mobile kitchen is one hell of an operation! I've gotten sort of bored with my duties at the shop, not to speak of the ignorance that prevails between **inmate**s and free staff alike. I feel the urge to move on now. I've had family members send in letters to request a hardship transfer, **INSHA-ALLAH!**" All of the family are doing well, **Al-HAMDULILLAH!** I talked to Dre yesterday. I talk to Mikal and Tony regularly; Mom, June, Reggie, Debbie, Angela, Berna Trisa, and Big Greg periodically. Once again, I've had the sheer joy of watching the Rock II do his thing on TV. I received a letter from Hakim Friday. (Smile). May **ALLAH** continue to watch over them all! Love and Peace...

It is football season again, and the brothers have had the pleasure of watching one of Washington's games on TV with me. Now, every Saturday we would huddle up in the TV room to watch Hakim and the Huskies compete. Hakim is a sophomore now, and appears to be in great shape this year! Mikal is finishing up his last season in Junior College, and anticipates transferring to a Division 1 College next year.

I enrolled in a correspondent course connected to Cal State University in Sacramento for Waste Water Treatment Operator, and engrossed myself in study and research again. I also began to spend as much time as possible in the Chapel, around the **Imam**. I began to lead the brothers in prayer when the **Imam** wasn't around. These men and I studied together, ate together, and challenged each other to increase our knowledge and insight. I also continued to send out greeting cards with poems in them like this one sent to all my sisters, called ***"SISTERS."***

"SISTERS"
It has been said that girls are sugar and spice
and everything nice, I also learned that you were
afraid of bugs, snakes, spiders and mice.
Yeah I know, I was a mischievous little Lad, amused
by your childhood fear, I can't imagine our family without you, each of you so dear.
Now look what time and nurturing has done, each
one of you lovely women, your love and support has been more like a good friend.
So what would be more appropriate than to honor you with poetic verse, for all the roles you've
played, like counselor, mentor and nurse.
Before the world I am delighted to declare, where
would we be without her? I thank **GOD** for June,
Debbie, Gloria and Angela, my **"SISTERS!"**
KBA

I began to think about my relationships, and involvement with girls and women over the years, having grown up in an era where men operated with double standards. As boys approached adolescence and began to exhibit a natural interest in girls, it was encouraged and even smiled upon, yet when girls exhibited the same natural curiosity, it was discouraged and in many cases, reprimanded. Although I got married at age twenty, I see and accept today, *that in some ways I was emotionally inept, confusing sex with love early in my development as a teenager.*

I thought about this, asked for forgiveness in prayer, then wrote this **poem:** *"FUTURE REFERENCE."*

"FUTURE REFERENCE"

As I reflect on the things we all thought were cool and hip, we were so naïve and ignorant about the value of companionship.
A young boy mimicking men in their games of wit and foreplay, rehearsing everything we saw those men do and even say.
Bragging rights in those circles of men, I'm the best there could be, taking for granted the awful consequences of that folly.
So much pain and confusion did result, an internal, agonizing hell, sexual conquests veiled her only real difference, female.
A spiritual unification of two, without her we are not whole, in dark, remote places, her precious gift was cunningly stole.
Inadvertent debasement caused by these acts of debauchery, by **GOD'S GRACE** I sat and pondered; what has become of me?
This isn't right, I can't possibly maintain all these women, not to think of the inevitable burdens from committing these sins.
Now here I am, no wife, no girlfriend, no woman, just these thoughts, reminisce, mistakes can only be used in a **"FUTURE REFERENCE."**
KBA

My father was an excellent example of loyalty and unwavering commitment to his wife and children. Yet he had a very stern and uncompromising stance on what he believed girls and boys should do and be about. Young people today would call this **old school or old fashioned.** I realized early on that our father was **homophobic** too. Now as a kid, I didn't even know that word existed. What I'm saying is that when our father saw things drifting far outside the norms in the media and in his travels in the late sixties and early seventies, he came home smashing on his boys! I distinctly remember my father preaching to me and my younger brothers about **the difference between femininity and masculinity!**

And if he saw us playing with one of our own sisters while she had a doll out playing with it, he would say: **boy go in there and get that G.I. Joe I bought you!** Now don't get it wrong please, I consider my father to be one of the greatest men I have ever had the pleasure and benefit of knowing and being mentored by! He shaped and molded me into a strong, **GOD CONSCIOUS** promulgator and provider that I have been and am today, and in many ways, **I am just like him. Yet in some ways through the process, I was damaged**! My father and mother raised nine children in the forties, fifties, sixties, seventies, and eighties in the Jim Crow era; Civil Rights era; and the Black Power Movement era, and yielded an influence over all of us that will always transcend time or place!

Amongst my peers, when we were eleven and twelve, we were not having sex! Back then, if a girl pulled her pants down and displayed her gifts to you through a glass window, it was something to run off and go tell the homies about! So you see, early on we were being conditioned to be **carnal creatures. I remember seeing so many transgressions and offenses against girls and women** *growing up*. Even from my own father. I have no idea what it is he was going through during those periods of his life.

I remember him saying to me later in life as an adult, that had it not been for his wife and children, the things he was exposed to while trying to support his family, **he would be dead or in prison!** One of the things he and his peers did to escape the horrors of that era was to drink liquor. Perhaps it was in those drunken stupors that he physically abused our mother. **I have vivid memories very young of my mother's screams when he did so**! Carnality is what eventually led my father to physically abuse me in a way that I said no man would ever do that to me again in life!

I am the same age as Michael Jackson. I grew up with the Jackson Five! When I was eleven and twelve, I and my two younger brothers had Afros like that of the Jackson Five, and on top of that, our older brother Reggie was skilled with the clippers, so he kept us lined up and groomed. During this time I remember our father chanting to us, I better not catch anyone of you boys coming home with your hair plaited or braided, because if I do, I promise you, **I'm going to kill you!** Well, this was a very pivotal time in my life. I was twelve, starting to smell things I didn't smell before. (Smile).

I was an honor student, a prerequisite to exist in my father's house! I was a multiple sport athlete long before Deon Sanders and Bo Jackson! I graduated from elementary school, headed to High school as the most likely to succeed in my class because I was class President. I had so many so-called girlfriends by the time I graduated from my elementary school. Yet it is always the one that got away, or pays you no attention that has a tendency to spark a heightened interest!

"Beyond Theze Wallz"

> "It seems that the lure of sexual attraction is
> that it harbors something forbidden!"
>
> ANONYMOUS

A young lady in my neighborhood that I grew up with, she blossomed into one of the most sculptured, naturally beautiful young ladies that I encountered in the neighborhood or at school! She was an academic scholar and a beast in track and field! Yet I believe she too grew up with some strict parameters about boys, because when she approached a boy or a group of boys, she would always have an expression on her face that seemed to be more rehearsed than natural. One day I corned her in the neighborhood, and asked her why she always looked mad or mean when she saw me? She smiled, and it was on after that! We walked and talked for hours. She was a real sprinter, quick a foot! So I would challenge her to runs, and when I tell you she could out run the average young man, believe me, she could!

So we start meeting each other after school almost every day, and one day, she asked me if I could come by her house Friday evening, because her parents are going to be leaving for the weekend and only she and her sister will be home. So of course I followed my *carnal* training and took her up on such a luscious invitation. When I arrived at her house, she was dressed in some pink nylon hot pants that look tight but are quite flexible, she was bare foot and her nails were perfectly manicured and painted a hot pink! Sharice was a caramel colored beauty with jet black hair, naturally curly all over her head!

Every time she got up her well defined muscles in her calves and thighs would move in sequence! And her eyes were like rich pearls that reflected light whether dim or bright! I was smitten! She asked me why I was smiling so much and that only made me smile more! You don't know? I'm in the presence of the prettiest young lady in Georgia! She smiled so hard I thought she would never stop! Then she leaned over and kissed me, and I kissed her back! I laid my head in her lap, and that was like placing my head at the heart of civilization! She ran her hand through that thick yet groomed lot on my head, and said: Baby, please let me be the only one that ever braids your hair, please.

I said you don't ever have to worry about that because I will never have my hair braided. She looked at me intently and said: why not? I sat up and said my father would without conscious or forethought, hesitation or reservation, **Kill Me**! She laughed so hard and said: you're kidding right? I said: no I am not! She said ok, then we cuddled up and watched a movie together, she popped popcorn and put a pizza in the oven. Once the movie ended, Sharice got up and went in her bedroom and came back with a comb, brush, grease and a hat.

She said: can I show you something? I said sure, go right ahead. She took that brush and brushed my hair upward, then she took that hat, pulled it down over my hair and stuffed my hair up in that hat. She said turn around, then she looked at me and said: You should go and take a look at yourself in the mirror. I got up and walked to the mirror and she came and stood behind me, she embraced me and said: you can't see any of your hair baby.

I looked at her and said: And? If you let me braid your hair, come over here baby, please sit on the floor, and I did. She said lean your back against the sofa. Then she sat on the sofa and placed my head squarely between those beautiful, well sculptured thighs and said: If you allow me to braid your hair, this is how I will do it, which means anytime you wish, you can rub my legs and kiss me. As weak as I was in that moment, I explained to Sharice again that I cannot go home to my father's house with my hair like that. She looked frustrated and said: doesn't your father work at night, and I replied: yes.

She said stay here with me until he leaves, then get up in the morning and take your hair down before he comes in. Then she said: It would mean so much to me Ken if I am the first girl to braid your hair, then she kissed me with fire and passion. I said ok; she leaped up from the sofa like she was startled by a spider and said: we are going to have so much fun together! She went in her bedroom and came out with this short silk mini-skirt on with no panties! I was so nervous, this was the closest I had ever come to having sex with a girl. I sat there, between her thighs, as she began to segment my hair, my stomach was in knots, because somehow I knew this would not turn out well.

After a while I loosened up and began to enjoy the position I was in with her, by rubbing her thighs and calves. She purred like a pet kitten while I did that. Before long, she was done. She asked me to go and look at what she had done to my hair in the mirror. I returned to the sofa with her, sat down next to her, took her in my arms and began to kiss her. As things heated up between us I began to rub all over her, even between her thighs. As I touched her precious garden I noticed that she would arch her back and start making noises I had never heard before! It reminded me of people speaking in tongues at Church!

We continued this exchange of touch and tease for a while until her older sister came out of her bedroom and said: Sharice! It's time for your company to go home! We jumped up like soldiers in the military, readjusted our clothes, kissed one more time, long and hard! We got up and she walked me to door, and said: thank you for a great evening, call me when get home ok. I said ok, kissed her one more time and walked down her driveway onto the street. I left her home walking on cloud nine! I smiled, danced and sang my way to the house. Sharice lived only a block away from our house so I was home in no time. As I approached our driveway, I stopped in my tracks! My father's car was still in the driveway, he didn't go to work! My father had worked at night for as early as I can remember. It was well pass the time for him to leave home, so he must not be going to work tonight.

As I stood one residence away looking at the driveway, I heard a voice in the dark call out my name: Kent…. Kent….I looked in the direction of the voice and my younger brother Dre, who was seven at this time had not come home before the street lights came on so he was in a world of trouble! Is this the reason my father did not go to work? As my brother Dre approached me he said pleadingly, **Kent please tell Bacadee I was with you, please!** I said boy, you are in trouble, and if I say you were with me, I too will be in trouble! As we stood there discussing this, the porch light flickered on and off several times and then the door opened, it was our father, standing in the doorway, signaling for the two of us to get in the house! As we both approached the porch with much trepidation, he opened the door and addressed my brother Dre first and said: where have you been? You know you were supposed to be home over an hour ago! My brother looked at me and said: I was with Kent!

I said no he wasn't! My father had a belt in his hand and began to strike my brother with it as he motioned for him to come in the house! He said you better not ever forget again about what time you are supposed to be in this house! My brother ran down the hallway crying and then my father's wrath turned on me. He said, whether he is with you, or whether he is not with you, if he is outside it is important that you be aware of where he is and what he is doing, you are the big brother!

Now get in this house right now! He struck me with the belt several times as I made my way to the hallway. As I maneuvered down the hallway, my father said boy take that hat off in my house! I said ok, and ran toward the bedroom and he said: hey! Come back here right now! As I turned around I knew right then, I was doomed! I walked slowly back to the dining room where my father and mother were, then he said take that hat off right now! I remember looking at my mother sadly, then I pulled that hat off my head. When I tell you that my father's eyes popped right out of their sockets and snapped back in, believe it! **He lost it!** He began to strike me with blows from his fists like an experienced boxer, laying head shots and uppercuts with the might of a grown man! I remember hearing my mother screaming and crying while telling my father: Arthur! Arthur! Stop it before you kill that boy!

My father struck me a few more times for good measure, and I fell down to the floor punch drunk! As the world spun around with me in a daze, my father stood me up and said something to me that has resonated with me for many years, haunting me in my sleep: ***Boy I have four girls and five boys and I be damned if I don't keep it that way***! Then he looked at my mother and said: ***Glo, (short for Gloria), go get me some scissors***! My mother pleaded with him, Arthur please! Haven't you done enough? What do you need scissors for Arthur? Please! He said it again with a force now that my mother clearly understood: Woman, I said go get me those scissors right now! My mother got up reluctantly, cried there and back with those scissors, and pleaded again, **Arthur, nooo…**

My father took those scissors and cut out those braids in my head in a way that left exposed scalp all over my head. As I watched my hair fall to the floor, I cried uncontrollably! After that, it was all over and he told me to get my behind ready for bed! As I made my way down that hallway, I had to steady myself by placing both hands on the walls to avoid falling. I climbed up on my bunk and there I would remain until my mother took me to the emergency room at the hospital a few days later. In that Malay, **my father had given me a concussion!** I couldn't eat or drink anything because it came right back up, and I had massive headaches! When it became apparent to my father what he had done, he sent me to the barber shop first, I had to have my head clean shaven and start from scratch, and from there to the hospital.

He told my mother on our way out the door, you tell those doctors that boy struck his head while playing football in the street, and she said ok… This would prove to be the incident that would create a schism between my father and me for years! I had already began to challenge any leadership/educators that supported curriculums of lies, at school and at home. This incident with my head happened over the summer between elementary and high school. I left elementary school an honor roll student, when high school began a few weeks later, I had already determined myself not to go, my hair hadn't even grown back yet! For the next three years, everything my father said do, **I didn't!** The beatings that resulted from my rebellion only toughened me, I became numb to them…

"What is a rebel? A man who says no!"

ALBERT CAMUS

In a crazy and bizarre way, that experience between my father and I liberated me! I did what I wanted to do without fear of retaliation or reprimand after that! **I had become hardened and I vowed that no man would ever do that to me again in life!** I even did something none of my siblings ever dared do, I ran away from home for about four months when I was fifteen. I was living with a den of prostitutes and their pimp, Smitty, right around the corner from my father's sister, Aunt Thelma. Now in hindsight I see that my rebellion hurt me more than it did my father. I stopped playing sports for a while and had to be retained a grade because of all the days I missed from school playing hooky. *I am just one of many cases I saw growing up, where talented/gifted young people fell victim to the dysfunction in their families and/or communities, and unlike myself, they never recovered!*

Another entry in my journal:

"AL-HAMDULILLAH!"
01-12-00........Wednesday

Well, oh journal, it's been a minute huh? Here we go! November 8th I went back to Riverside County for re-sentencing. That fantastic family of mine hired a charismatic attorney to see if we could get the D.A. and Judge to agree on a different sentencing choice after Mr. Ed

Daire filed some new motions for me. It was a noble effort that fell short of its intended mark. I did get 118 days credit that was due along with the original sentence of 8 years and 4 months. That whole out to court experience was a real test of character and a potent reminder of how perpetual crime and sentencing is in this Police State. I was blessed to see Tony, Hakim, and Rochelle while I was in court, and Tony and Momma paid me a visit while I was at the Murrieta facility.

    I spoke with Artie, June, Debbie, Diane, Reggie, Berna, Angela, Rasheedah, Kenya and Alexandria on the telephone the night of Hakim's (Washington's) football game against UCLA. I saw that game in the county too, it was a good game, Washington loss in overtime. I witnessed a real riot in Riverside County jail Thanksgiving night, and that was wild!

    I returned to CMC in time to participate with my brothers in observing the **Fast of Ramadhan, "ALLAH-U-AKBAR!"** Oh yeah, I met Mr. Ricci in person, that was a trip! Here we are, in the year 2000, five years ago it seemed like a distant star, yet here it is! Three more years and I'm homeward bound! (Smile)!

CHAPTER 10

"RELEASE IN SIGHT"

*"Difficulties break some men but make others.
No axe is sharp enough to cut the soul of a
sinner who keeps on trying, one armed with
the hope that he will rise until the end."*

NELSON MANDELA

ANOTHER EXCELLENT EXAMPLE of **GOD'S limitless mercy and grace**, and one of the primary reasons why my errant adolescent behavior was put in check, is when my oldest sister June, met and eventually married *Gregory Bennett,* loving known to all of us as *Big Greg*. By this time, my father had already told me he was done whipping on me; that he was tired, that he had three more children younger than me, and he needed to conserve his efforts and energy for them. Big Greg was a stalwart, red Black man that has an amazing story of his own! He was raised in one of the toughest Government projects in Atlanta, **Perry Homes.**

He was raised by the type of strong Black woman that doesn't exist anymore, Big C! When he began dating my sister, he took an interest in me right away, taking the time to find me in the neighborhood whenever he came to our home. He saw I had a fondness for basketball, and would stop on the court in the neighborhood to shoot around with us while he talked to me. Then he invited me to come and hang out with him and my sister on weekends because he played basketball most weekends when it wasn't football season, because he played Semi-Pro football, all of this in addition to working ten hour shifts at General Motors! Before long we were inseparable! I spent many weekends with my sister and Big Greg during school, and the whole summer with them when I was out of school. I baby sat with my niece Trisa whenever they wanted to go out, she was only two or three at the time, and otherwise, it was Big Greg and me hanging out, swimming, playing basketball or wrestling with each other all over the house; we tore up some of the furniture slamming each other all over the place! He taught me so much! *And whenever I hung out with him, he required me to carry myself like a G, even though I was still a kid.*

Big Greg, Johnathan (Buck) and June at his High school graduation.

Older siblings Lil Greg and Trisa, proud of their Lil Bro. Buck.

One of the realest men I had encountered ever! For example, one evening when I was fifteen he came to me and said, I want to hang out with my wife alone for a while, don't you have somewhere to go? And I said no! He said well you need to find somewhere to go, here are the car keys. I said I don't know how to drive yet, he said you will by the time you get back, see you later! So I left driving this huge boat of a car, one of those old four door Chryslers! (Smile). On the weekends we would pack a cooler, and make sandwiches, because on Saturday morning, we would drive around from one outdoor court to another, all over Atlanta, playing basketball together! We wouldn't make it back home until after dark!

I credit this one man with being a game changer in my life! By the time I was sixteen I already began to change and graduated from high school with 4.0 GPA. We have remained the best of friends and brothers to this day! I returned to the yard excited about being back. After I got situated, I made my way to the Chapel, to make prayer and catch up with all of the brothers. As I entered the Chapel, I thought my eyes were deceiving me! I saw Mustafa, seated next to the brother Rasheed, conversing as I walked in! Man when I say that was one of those moments in life you know for sure that **GOD** is always in control, this was one of those! They jumped up and embraced me like I had been their long lost love one that they didn't know if they would ever lay eyes on again! And I felt the same way!

Mustafa's custody level dropped and he requested CMC, and they sent him here! We laughed so hard because I said CMC must be short of rebel rousers! So we got to do the ***Fast of Ramadhan*** together. We have been informed by ***Imam Kamal*** that this year we will be able to spend a whole night off prison grounds together during the ***Night of Power! The Imam also began to enhance his efforts with all of us by having other Imams like Ron El-Amin, the Chaplain at Chino State prison come in for the EID's and other events. And other anointed men of GOD that speak to the heart and soul of men in prison and on the streets.*** Mustafa filled me in on all he had gone through since we last saw each other. I took on a great hobby on the yard, woodworking. I learned how to make custom clocks and jewelry boxes, and I began to send those out to all of my relatives. I sent out heart shaped jewelry boxes to all the females in my family.

I made custom clocks for my mother and father too. I continued to write poetry, and send them out to my family, like this one I sent to my aunt and uncle for their 50th wedding anniversary: ***"JAMES AND RUTH!"***

"JAMES AND RUTH"

As I look at this beautiful picture that the two of you sent
me, of the two of you together on your 50th anniversary.
I closed my eyes and in instant, my mind reflected, on
the love and warmth over the years that you directed.
A radiant smile and gentle words, what a unique lady, young
women today could take a lessons from you Auntie.
A legend! You met the challenges to raise your family, often I think of the bond Uncle, between you and Bacadee.
I would get excited whenever my cousins came over to
play, or we loaded up the car and on Holly St. we'd stay.
The barbeques, the dinners, cakes, and Brunswick stew;
kickball, hide and go see; the adults played Tripoly too.
Yes, these vivid memories are a constant inspiration, bringing joy to my heart even in the darkest situation.
You're two very special people, **"GOD"** knows
that this is the truth, thanks for the card and token, I love you **"JAMES AND RUTH!"**
KBA

Dedicated to the love and memory
of Ruth and James Momon

Mr. and Mrs. Ruth and James Momon on their 50th Wedding Anniversary... *GOD bless you!*

I wasn't back at CMC but about six weeks when I was called to the office and told to roll all my property up, when I asked why, they said you're headed back to the County jail. They never tell you why you're going back if you don't already know, and you have no choice in the matter. I wasn't in the county two days when the assistant D.A. and one of his henchmen came to pay me a visit. They informed me that my crime partner, the one that committed the bank robbery with me, he had been a fugitive all this time, had been apprehended.

Apparently he got busted coming back into the States from Mexico with a lot of marijuana. He had changed his entire appearance, changed his name and had I.D. to support his assumed identity. The problem is, when they fingerprinted him, bells and whistles went off everywhere! So as I listened attentively, they said if I don't cooperate with them in identifying him he will walk, because, all the original witnesses in our case can't be located, it's been five years. I looked at the two of them and said: you brought me all this way, back down here to share that with me?

They said it is not fair for you to take responsibility for your actions and go away like you have for five years and him being free all of this time. I sat back in my chair and looked at both of them, pondering to myself about this whole angle that they have with me and their office. The fact is, they don't care about me or any other defendant that they have prosecuted! I saw so many uneducated or uninformed men that got railroaded by accepting **plea bargains** in cases that had absolutely no merits! All they care about is **conviction rates,** that's how they measure their performance! I told them that outstanding case is strictly between your office, and the guy you picked up, it has nothing to do with me!

I would appreciate it you if guys put me back on the first thing smoking to C.M.C. so I can finish doing my time! They said ok, but if he gets released, it's on you! I laughed, got up and returned to my pod. Two days later, they came back to visit me and said we had to let him go, hope you're happy, and I said I know you're not! As a retaliatory act toward me for my lack of cooperation, they lost me in the system on purpose! I should have been back at C.M.C. months earlier, yet I lingered in the squalor of the County jail. In this facility there is no outside yard, every activity is enclosed, even the court where we played basketball. To break the monotony many of us played basketball.

You had to play basketball bare foot on that rubber floor because the flap japs we had to wear didn't provide any traction. My last week there, while playing ball, a guy snatched a rebound and landed on my foot! I heard the bone crack when he landed on my foot, and I watched my toe inflate like a balloon right before my eyes! Now I have a real dilemma, if I report this so I can get some semblance of treatment or pain medicine, it is grounds for them to keep me in the County even longer. So I opted to tuff it out, walk on my heel and not my toes. It was a painful process, but I managed. And sure enough, a week later, I was hopping onto a bus headed back to C.M.C... This next entry in my journal puts it in perspective:

"BISMILLAH IR RAHMAN IR RAHIM"
09-24-00
Sunday

Wow! First of all, I must apologize to you my dear journal! It's been eight months since my last entry. Shortly after my last entry, I was whisked back to the county jail in Riverside. I didn't make it back to CMC until June! That experience in the county proved to be another real test for me! I was blessed to see my sons, Tony and Sonya, my nieces Destinee' and Diamond, Debbie, Rochelle, and my very first grandbaby, Raquel. The real homie Jeff, came to see me too. I made some acquaintances, Cuda and Din-boy. They have written me since I returned. Cuda is on the streets and Din-boy is headed to the Pen. All of the brothers and Imam Kamal were glad that I made it back unscathed.

"**AL-HAMDULILLAH!**" I stopped off briefly in Chino, got to hang out with some of the Muslims there. I also ran into Matthew, one of my ole cellmates from the county. Now that I'm back, preparations are being made to utilize the last stretch of this time, (28 months), to my advantage. I hope to leave here with at least an Associate's degree. It's football season, and once again, I'm delighted to witness Hakim do his thing on National TV... Mikal has persevered and now he too is at Washington and due to be showcased this weekend, (9-30-00)...**GOD** be with those boys in their endeavors. Rasheedah and Kenya are still unsettled. I haven't heard from them in a while. **We loss Ms. McKibbens in July, GOD have mercy on her...**

Article posted in the Press Enterprise in Riverside about the boys and me, the close relationship we have maintained even from prison, and possible Rose Bowl implications for the Washington Huskies.

Upon return to the yard, I got right back to my ***program,*** studying and worshipping daily, working and working out. By this time Mustafa only a little more than a year left on his prison sentence, so went spent as much time around each other as we could. Its football season again, and by now everyone, prison staff and most of the ***inmates*** knew about my sons playing football at Washington, so even the officers would stop by the TV room to watch games with us. Washington was off to a great start, going undefeated for much of the season. ***Then when Washington played against Stanford, Hakim's roommate, Curtis Williams, the one guy that protected the secondary with Hakim by laying hits that matched Hakim's defensive prowess! These two guys were ferocious, nothing got pass the two of them in that secondary together! Curtis attempted to tackle a running back for Stanford and fractured his neck! He had to be carted off the field on a stretcher! I turned away from the TV and prayed for that young man and his family! Washington finished their regular season 10-1, and were headed to Rose Bowl against Drew Brees and Purdue.***

Before the Rose Bowl game, Hakim came to visit with me. He seemed apprehensive and subdued in thought during the visit, then he said: ***Dad, I know how you feel about education, and I want to finish school, yet I am very concerned about staying for my senior year, or forfeiting my senior year and declaring myself eligible for the NFL Draft this year. You saw what happened to Curtis; that could have be, or could be next year! I think I should leave while my stock is high.*** I told Hakim that you must make the choices that are best for you and your life.

I will respect whatever the choice is, the choice is yours' to make. He seemed relieved as our visiting time came to a close. I hugged him intently, told him I love him, and then said have your best game ever in that Rose Bowl! After that visit, I had a slew of reporters and journalists visit me at CMC, to see if I would confirm for them and their readers, whether Hakim would stay another year, his senior year, or would he declare himself eligible for the draft. I was amused by all of the attention, yet said that they must allow Hakim to reveal to them what his choice is, not me. Another historic entry in my journal:

> "BISMILLAH IR RAHMAN IR RAHIM"
> 12-24-00
> Sunday
>
> Greetings dear journal, a few months have passed since I spoke with you last. Another year has come and nearly gone in here. It has been a very busy year, on and off the prison yard, for me and the family. Andre has moved out here to California. I am very proud of him that he has made up his mind to get back to being his very best. **"ALL PRAISES ARE DUE TO ALLAH!"** He does seem at a point in his life where constructive change is inevitable. Ms. Kenya just arrived here Wednesday, (Smile)... I'm so glad that **"ALLAH"** blessed me with those big boys, her Big brothers! They took it upon themselves to send for their little sister. I hope to speak with her in a few days. Well, the boys are gearing up for the Big Rose Bowl, the Washington Huskies went 10-1 this season, (Smile)... Hakim had a great season, and Mikal has played this entire season with Washington. Tony, Dre, and the boys sent me a very nice package a couple of weeks ago. May **"ALLAH"** bless them all! The next entry will be 2001, may **"ALLAH"** continue to watch over us all...

I spoke with my brother Reggie today, we laughed and talked about everything, and of course he and the whole family are on pins and needles about the Rose Bowl. Many of them are coming out here for the game. I gave this brother a nickname that I have used exclusively for years, *Joe Beavers*. So after our telephone conversation, I went back to the dorm and penned this poem for him that describes our relationship over the years: *"JOE BEAVERS!"*

"JOE BEAVERS"

With this time on my hands, often I reminisce
about us, and our family; my earliest memories are when you were eight and I was three.
Smiles and laughter are aroused as I think of the
things we did and said, childhood games, silly nick-
names, and quiet time on our bunkbeds.
There was nothing lacking or left to be desired at
ole three sixty-five, Sunday dinners, frappe, holiday feasts, and Bacadee was no jive!
I recall you in your baseball uniform when you
played for Mr. Blake; sand lock football in the back
yards, on defense you were hard to shake!
In High school on the honor roll, an asset in the
Marching Band; a standard bearer; a leader; always offering a compassionate hand.
A prodigy of the volatile sixties; you worked to be
your very best; when the school curriculum fell
short, you guys created Black Awareness!
What a profound impact you had on me; styl-
ish attire, with a neat cut afro; a mind so sharp and
alert, just ask Reggie, he will always know.

Like so many young men of that era, your life was
not without trials; I thought about Byrd, Marvin,
Monk, Lil Pace, they were with us awhile.
How close we both came too, to returning to that
from which we came; brushes with death that made
it clear to us, something had to change.
Soul stirring fireplace moments, and drinking sprees
in the park; as we shared our views and experiences from afternoon till long after dark.
We were always there for one another, no matter the time or place; the love that I have for you
my brother, no time or distance can erase!
I had to put these thoughts in stanza, by word
of mouth few would believe us; that these real
life trials and triumphs belong to you:

"JOE BEAVERS!"

KBA

HAPPY NEW YEAR!! 2001!!! "ALL PRAISES ARE DUE TO ALLAH!" The brothers and I did a magnificent spread together! I have entered into a brand new year with so many things to be grateful for, especially from here! So many issues and concerns have gone on, and still go on with those that I will die for without question, *my love ones,* that I still have to mitigate from here! *And in a number of the cases, I knew if I had been on the streets, things would have turned out much different!* Some of the same roles and responsibilities with my folks that I at times felt burdened or overwhelmed by, the **LORD** now allows me to see clearly what it is like without me being there, due to my confinement...

I also realize that what had been proffered me early on in this journey proved to be true. The **LORD** had placed and kept so many great mentors in my sons' lives, in my absence. **Unsung heroes:** Like **Gus**! Gus and I met when I first came to California. I wasn't out here three weeks and I was headed to a job interview on the Riverside Transit Authority, The bus, and there was this brother in the back of the bus that was uncommonly friendly, engaging everybody seated near him in conversation. I said to myself, he's not from out here. I detected a Southern drawl and mannerisms, and sure enough, he's from Mississippi.

Well fate would have it that we got off the bus at the same stop, starting talking and haven't stopped to this very day! As a matter of fact, I met big **Bob** through Gus a couple of weeks later, *and the three of us remained the best of friends until the untimely passing of big Bob two years ago.* When I prepared to send for my boys two months after I moved out here, Gus was the brother that encouraged and supported my efforts with them. Gus is the kind of brother that is connected to everything, on both sides of the law! When I was a fugitive, on the run is this case, Gus is the brother I ran too, and he put a covering of protection over me until I decided what direction I needed to go in. He told me not to worry about the boys before I got sentenced, that he would look after them like his own boys, and he did!

Checking on them both whether at school and at home, making sure that they do the right things. I will always be indebted to him, and my sons approaching their forties now, call him Uncle Gus. While in High school, (Riverside Poly), they would encounter a dynamic brother that became an assistant coach for the football team that both of them played on named *Jeff Andrews*. He saw the raw talent in both of them and began to mentor them on the field, in the weight room and at home. Once he realized the boys had dreams of making it to the NFL, he challenged them to stay focused and he would introduce them to current and former NFL football players, one being his own cousin, **Claudius Wright**.

Once they met Claudius, he and Jeff adopted these boys as little brothers, exposing them to NFL events and players, and providing them with the kind of accountable behavior that only big brothers can demand! This influence would help carry them into college and beyond! I have had visits from Jeff and Claudius, and speak to them regularly. I thank **GOD** for these brothers! My boy ***Terry Goldston*** in Atlanta, lifelong friends and comrades we are! Terry is originally from Tennessee. I met him at the HR office of the American Red Cross, we both got hired as drivers on the same day in the late-eighties and we have seen each other through great times and many trials.

A rare friendship that is time honored, ***sacred!*** Terry remembers when the dream of athletic excellence with my sons was born back home in Atlanta, because he and I were around each other when our children were small. When I was on the run from the F.B.I., I slid in under the veil of darkness to consult with my boy about what I had done and what's next. This is the same brother that drove my mother and me to the Bus depot, to see me off to California. ***My Folks!*** My Big cousin ***Wayne Momon***, we were raised together like brothers because his mother and mine were each other's only sibling. He has been and remains a lifelong friend and mentor, and is one of my primary spiritual gurus.

Greg Jones, married to my older sister Deborah many years ago. An academic scholar that help shape and mold me as a young man. And so, so many others in the family and communities in California and Atlanta that were obviously sent to fill that hole left by my absence, to see these fellows through their transitions, like the **Luginbills**, a beautiful family in Riverside that took my boys into their home, supported and helped nurture them like their own kids. **The Tavalones**, another wonderful family in Riverside that took a personal interest in the boys before I got sentenced, their son **Nick** attended High school with the boys.

And the **Edmonds**, they helped look out for Kenya while the boys were in Washington, **GOD** bless you! I have spoken to and had visits with my sons and the Luginbills. *Another amazing example of GOD'S influence with all of us, and what a small world it really it is: I met the maternal grandfather of my two youngest granddaughters at C.M.C., (Mr. (Junebug) Spratt), long before our adult children met, and neither one of us had anything to do with them meeting each other!* I sat in a trance like state, pondering over these real evidences for a while, that the promises of the **LORD** are really true!

Well, today is the day! **Big Rose Bowl Game!!** I'm so excited with and for my sons and Huskie Football! It won't be an easy victory because Purdue is a worthy opponent, they have an All-American quarterback named Drew Brees, so they have to play smart ball! I believe I will see the largest congregation of *inmates* and prison staff in the dorm around the TV room today for this game! I know we are putting together huge spreads with all the other compliments to go with them for this game. I busied myself with cleaning and other preparations until it was time to shower. By the time I got dressed, brothers began to flock into the dorm, Mustafa leading the way.

We went into the TV room, put the TV on the channel for the game and the Pre-game Rose Bowl show was on. *I learned then that this game would be dedicated to Curtis Williams, all of the players had his number on their jerseys, and Curtis was shown in a wheelchair with a jersey on, in a glass booth with his family. A very emotional moment for all the coaches and team mates!* As the TV room began to fill with men from different walks of life, and we prepared for kick-off, the energy in that TV room could light up the Rose Bowl! It was a competitive game, yet Purdue's offense was no match for Washington's defense! Hakim had nine solo tackles in that game, and I got to see both my boys play, and raise their helmets in victory after the game! *The final score was 34-24 Washington!*

Mikal and Hakim raising their helmets in victory after the Rose Bowl in Pasadena, Ca.-January 1, 2001.

After that Rose Bowl game, Hakim made it official, announcing to the media that he is going to forego his last year of school to enter into the NFL Draft, and the same week, I read it in bold print in the Seattle Post: ***"Hakim Akbar is foregoing his senior year to enter the NFL Draft to help his family!"*** Mikal has another year of eligibility at Washington so he is staying. Several weeks later I spoke with Mikal and Claudius, they expressed concerns with me about Hakim preparing himself properly for the NFL Combines, so he can showcase his talents at the highest level. Hakim had already secured a Sports Management company and Agent. I assured them that I would speak to Hakim as soon as I can about this. A few days later, I spoke with Hakim about his necessary preparation for the NFL Combines and other concerns, he assured me he will be ready. Another entry from the journal:

"BISMILLAH IR RAHMAN IR RAHIM"
04-09-01
Monday

Hi journal. (Smile)... Time for another entry. Time is really moving right along. Before long it will be the year 2002, and I, **(GOD willing)**, can finally exhale, and myself a long, good cry, preferably while soaking in a hot calgon scented bath! Everything seems to be going according to schedule. I'm presently enrolled in the Operator in training program. As soon as the weather becomes a bit more stable, (warmer and sunny), I'll get on, or back on my strict exercise regimen. I spoke with Ms. Kenya, Hakim, Dre, Tony, Sonya, and one of homeboys from Atlanta, big Dale. I also spoke with Debbie, Reggie, Big Greg, Buck, and my beautiful mother! Everyone seems to be fine. Well,

> all of the immigrants, (new Californians), are headed to Atlanta for a big NFL Draft party for Hakim. I'm anxious to see who picks him up too. Mikal is on crutches, he tore his knee up in Spring Camp with Washington! We are all wishing him a speedy recovery! May **GOD** continue to keep us all safe and blessed.

Several brothers, and prison staff too, watched as Hakim got drafted by the New England Patriots. I spoke with him later, and although he was happy to be selected, he wasn't that excited about playing football in that region of the country where it gets really cold during football season, and being so far away from all of his folks.... I congratulated him, and told him how proud I was of him!

> "Success is not final, failure not fatal, it is
> the courage to continue that counts."
>
> WINSTON CHURCHILL

During this time of the year, Imam Kamal Abdul Jabbar began to have regular talks with us in the Chapel, before and after Jumah prayer and Taleems. His passion as Imam and Chaplain toward all of us far exceeded his office and title! He really began to challenge the psychology of crime and criminality, and made it clear to us that we were insane, and now that we have been restored to sanity, not arrested but rescued; what are we to do now? That crime can never be an option to any of us again, because the only thing any man in here can ask for, is one more shot, one more opportunity to get it right! The Imam spent extra time with me, grooming me to lead the Taleems, and even Jumah prayer whenever he could not make it into the prison on time for this service.

Today I have been informed that I'm being considered for a unique program at the Firehouse outside the prison gates, and I will need to get dressed because the Captain of the Firehouse will be picking me up and taking me down there for an interview. I showered and got dressed, then waited at the gate for the Captain to pick me up. After about fifteen minutes, a guy approached the outside of the gate, as he got closer he looked at me and smiled, then asked me if my name is Kenneth Akbar, and I said yes. An officer came out of the office by the gate, told me to turn around, searched me, then he unlocked the gate. The other guy extended his hand and introduced himself as Captain Greene, and then said let's go.

I walked outside the prison gates, looking behind me as the officer locked the gate behind me. I followed Captain Greene down the hill to an official Fire Dept. truck, we jumped in and he drove down the hill. I looked on curiously as we drove away. I had been outside the prison grounds many times with the California Department of Forestry, but this was different. As we approached the gate to drive outside the prison, Captain Greene made a U-turn right in front of an official Firehouse! What memories swarmed me as we pulled up! I joined the Fire Dept. in Atlanta when I was twenty-one years old. Much of my youth, my first careers were in Public Safety. Many of my siblings went directly to colleges/universities after High school. *I do accept today that I am an extremist… Whenever I committed myself to doing good, I did extremely good!*

Whenever I have committed myself to doing bad, I did extremely bad! After those years of rebellion with my father, I made a complete about face. I was so responsible at age sixteen that my father began to entrust me with the use of the extra vehicle at the house. I met my wife in High school when I was sixteen, and told her when we met that I am looking for a wife that I can build a family with. When I graduated from High school I went straight to work, to fund my dreams, and to get out of my father's house.

My first job was in security, from there to law enforcement, a graduate of two Police Academies, City of Atlanta being one of them, and Firefighting also in the City of Atlanta. That influence came directly from my oldest brother Artie, who was a Lieutenant with Atlanta Fire Dept. at that time. *One of the great ironies of my own personal story, and a landmark experience, driving home why perseverance and faith is critical when facing the storms in our lives is this: the day I got sentenced to state prison, my brother Tony received a letter in the mail from Riverside County Sheriff's Department saying I was hired*! I had gone through the whole hiring process, the background check, physical agility test, several interviews and written exams, *and all I needed to do was be patient and continue to persevere in the face of adversity in faith and constancy....*

> "The two top habits that will decide between success and failure, between real change and staying in the same place are patience and perseverance."
>
> MARK REKLAU

So when we pulled up in front of that Firehouse, I reflected on my experiences at Firehouse Number Two, in Southwest Atlanta, off Jonesboro Road. I lived there for two years, as a Firefighter. As we entered the Firehouse, I noticed other **inmates** seated around the Firehouse, about eight of them, I nodded in passing and continued to follow the Captain to his office. Once there, he had me have a seat across from his desk as he pulled out my file before speaking with me. He said the reason that I, and your counselor on the yard brought you down here is because you are eligible to live and work here, as a real Firefighter and EMT... I saw in your file that you were a Firefighter on the streets, in Atlanta right? Yes sir. I will need to get some information from you regarding your service there, and there are stacks of forms I will need you to fill out for me.

Before that, let me share with you some of the pros and cons about being here at this Firehouse. It is only eleven **inmates** down here at any time. You guys have separate bunks and lockers just like Firefighters on the street. All of you will be required to go through real Fire Academy training, and EMT training. Some of your training will be here, and some of it off-site. Once we get you guys trained properly we are going to become a part of the Tri-County DECON Response Team and will respond to actual incidents on the streets. In addition to this, you guys will alternate on the ambulance out there in the bay, for the East Wing and West Wing of the prison.

That's the whole prison! Responding to incidents on the yards, with a stretcher to transport patients to the Hospital on the East yard if necessary. The challenge for all of you is this, this is a brand new program, and you guys are pioneers. The liberties, accommodations, and meals will be many days like that on the streets, and you guys will be interfacing with free people, sometimes when we're not around. We are having this necessary talk with all of you, because we need somebody amongst you to take the lead, and keep the rest in check, always. Because if there is one incident with the public, not only is it going to make the papers, programs like these will become non-existent! All of the certifications you guys are going to get, are State certs that can be used on the streets when you get out.

So what do you think? Tell you what, let's go meet the rest of the guys before you tell me what you think. The guys were in two separate areas of the Firehouse lounging in front TVs, a laid back group of guys that seemed content to be where they are; they extended their hands and introduced themselves, and asked if I was going to join them down here and I said yes. The Captain looked at me and smiled. Then he took me back up to the prison yard and said I will be moving down there this week, so get my things ready. I thanked him for the opportunity as he escorted me back to the gate where an officer was waiting.

As I arrived back on the yard, I washed up and made prayer, then I went out on the yard to find Mustafa and Rasheed, to meet with them and other brothers, to let them know I will be moving to the Firehouse. Time flew down there at that Firehouse! With all of the training and drilling, at the Firehouse, and off-site with other local Fire Depts. It was challenging and I loved it! The most impactful experiences, often sad experiences was on that ambulance we all had to take different shifts on, **twenty four hours a day!** I had never been over to the East yard before moving to the Firehouse. The East yard is **Supermax,** the **Big House,** where the real insanity exists! Lifers that are never going home, young and old, and others with lengthy prison sentences!

The Hospital for the prison is also located there and so many men are housed there with diseases and disorders, right along with the emotionally and mentally insane! Many times whenever we had to transport someone to the Hospital, we had to wait on the yard by the Hospital, seated right outside waiting for the stretcher to put it back on the ambulance. The things we saw daily, men being escorted in wheelchairs and on foot, with their faces strapped up with facial restraints, because they have a history of biting officers, or they are Aids patients that are spitters, because they have spit on officers before! A half dozen officers surrounded them as they escorted them to and fro!

All of the Drag queens and Transvestites were on the East yard! Men prancing around like women, nearly breaking their hips to get the attention of other men! I saw cases right before my eyes where some of the lifers had made these other men their lovers, and would check them on the yard about prancing around like that and demanded that they return to the cell right now! There are two floors in the Hospital that housed mental patients, after the closure of a lot of Mental Health facilities in California, the prisons got many of those patients! I responded to calls on the East yard day and night! One call, the brother had lost it! Gone! Ramming his head against the cell door until he was bleeding profusely!

I responded to three separate incidents with lifers that will always stand out in my mind! One of them, this brother came in when he was twenty years old, now at fifty-four, and right after going before the parole board and being denied freedom again, he decided to end it by cutting both wrists, not before writing a letter explaining why he did it... **He could not do it anymore! And one lifer just died of old age, he had an A to start his CDC number, and mine was a J!** We responded to the aftermath of riots on the East and West yards, and had to do Triage with the number of injuries **inmates** sustained during those acts of violence! **It was insane,** I got tired on that ambulance after a while, and gained enough rank to trade chores with less senior guys! The fellows and

"Beyond Theze Wallz"

I got to follow Hakim and the New England Patriots right into the Super Bowl! Yeah! **What a ride!**

"The best way out is always through!"

ROBERT FROST

The very night that the Patriots won the Conference final, headed to the Super Bowl, my son Hakim flipped his Escalade during in climate weather, traveling too fast and lost control, rolling his vehicle several times! He was thrown out of the vehicle as it rolled and he was thrown into a patch of woods on the side of the roadway; it took Paramedics a while to find him! Officers came down to the Firehouse to get me because my family notified the prison. When they came to get me I knew something was wrong, they wouldn't tell me anything except that the Lieutenant wants to see me.

They escorted me into his office and I sat down. He had the officers close the door as they exited. Then he told me your son has been in a horrible car accident, I don't know his condition. I am about to call your family on my phone to allow you to speak with them, I believe it was your brother I spoke with, and I'm sorry and hope it's not too bad. I thanked him as he called my brother Tony. He handed me the receiver as the phone rang. Tony answered with a crackling in voice and said he is so sorry, and he knew he needed to contact me because they need me to pray along with them that he will be fine.

Right now he is in ICU, we don't know the full extent of his injuries big Brother, but he's busted up pretty bad! The prison staff told us they will allow you to communicate with us as we find things out ok, I love you man! *We prayed on the phone together then he hung up. I sat there numb I believe for ten minutes are so, I didn't remember the Lieutenant asking me if I was alright and him saying to me that he will give me some time alone. I cried for a few minutes, for my son and my family, then I cried to the LORD imploring HIS mercy and grace, right now.*

After a while the Lieutenant came back, sat down and said: protocol requires that we to take you off the Firehouse assignment until this difficult involving your family gets better, and I said ok. He asked me if there is any dorm I would like to stay in temporarily and I said yes, I chose the dorm Mustafa was in.

It had to be around two-thirty in the morning when the officer escorted me into that dorm, he had to turn his flashlight on when we got to my bunk, it happened to be right across from Mustafa's Bunk. *He was awakened by the light and noise. He raised up and said: Akbar, is that you? I said yes brother Mu. He said what happened? I gestured for him to follow me away from the beds so we don't wake up everybody, and I explained what happened, he looked at me, and said I will be right back. He went and got dressed, then we both washed up and prayed together for hours until daybreak!*

Later that morning, as everyone awakened and turned on the TVs, it was on the news: **"Standout football player right out of Southern California, Rose Bowl champion with the Washington Huskies, and rookie with the Super Bowl bound New England Patriots, Hakim Akbar was seriously injured in a car accident near Boston in the early morning hours, his condition is considered serious but stable."** For the next few days, everywhere I went, prison staff and everyone else went out of their way to come over and tell me that they heard what happened, and they are praying for me and the family.

The **Imam** called me to the Chapel because he too had seen the news and spoke with brothers about it. He offered me his unwavering support, and asked if there is anything I needed him to do. He also got approval for me to use the phone in the Chapel to call family as needed. Hakim remained in ICU for three weeks before he began to show improvement, during that time he lost seventy pounds!

> "Overcoming what frightens you the most, strengthens you the most!"
>
> MATSHONA DHLIWAYO

> "So verily with hardship there is relief, verily with the hardship there is relief."
>
> QURAN 94: 5-6

Another journal entry:

"BISMILLAH IR RAHMAN IR RAHIM"
01-27-02

Well, another New Year has been commemorated from behind these gates. It is truly a blessing to be able to say that after all this time, (seven years), "I go home next year!"

"AL-HAMDULILLAH!" (Smile). So much has transpired since my last entry! My mother; my sisters Debbie and June, Tony and my niece Carmen Tia visited with me during the Thanksgiving Holiday. They all look so, so good great! Hakim's football team, the Patriots, started out slow, losing. They began to focus and win!

Then the first week of December, I had the scare of my life since being incarcerated! Hakim rolled his SUV in New England and nearly killed himself! By **GOD'S grace**, he is recovering well and is willfully determined to get back to his athletic pursuits. In the meantime the Patriots are playing in the Super Bowl next week. Mikal is studying hard at UW, and says he is ready to crack some heads next season! Ms. Kenya is sounding so much like a grown lady, it's scary! We don't know where or what is going on with Rasheedah. **GOD help us all......**

It took both those boys of mine, now stalwart, strong young men, a year to rehabilitate their injuries! Both of them went on to play football again at the highest level! The Patriots went on to win that Super Bowl, by the way. I start hanging out a lot more on the yard with my boy! Mustafa! His date to be released is rapidly approaching, next month! ***"ALL PRAISES ARE DUE TO GOD!"*** I finally got to meet his father in the visiting room, **(Eugene Zeke Watts). (Pops)…**

Eugene Zeke Watts (Pops) and his proud son/Mustafa Shabazz

"HAPPY BIRTHDAY POPS"

What standard can we use to measure a parent's love?
Their patience and guidance must be sent from above!
What care and attention it really takes to nurture a child.
What discipline it takes to keep them all in rank and file.
Sometimes we take for granted the sacrifices they made.
The very hard work that went into keeping the bills paid.
Depriving themselves of basic things so we would not.

Making sure we were well fed before scrapping the pots. Just a few compelling reasons why I love you a whole lot! I'm thinking of you always, **HAPPY "BIRTHDAY POPS!"**
KBA

Dedicated to the loving memory of Eugene Zeke Watts

He came on Saturday, and was so honored to meet me, and he wouldn't stop thanking me for the influence I had with his son. I looked at Mustafa, and we both smiled! Mustafa and I spent the succeeding weeks going over his own list of priorities and how he would address and accomplish them. We prayed a lot for the next few weeks and before we knew it was here, time to go...... The journal describes that day perfectly!

07-02-02
"WITH THE NAME OF ALLAH, THE BENEFICENT, THE MERCIFUL!"
Today serves as a day of real honorable mention! My dear brother, my comrade of cell 152, my advisor and confidant throughout almost the entirety of this prison sojourn, Marcus (Mustafa Muhammad Shabazz) Wilborn went home to his family today, he paroled. "ALL PRAISES ARE DUE TO ALLAH!"

Six months to the house and two unexpected things happened to me. One is Terri got in touch with me, she wrote me a letter. I hadn't heard from her in years! We stopped communicating before I left Tehachapi. I thank **GOD** for helping me to make a very difficult decision about her and me. She was very forthwith and candid with me and I do appreciate that. I had five years left to do and she was on the streets. *She told me there are needs that she has that I can't possibly satisfy from here. I got it and liberated her and me by severing communication between us. I had seen so many arguments and fights occur between men that had nothing to do with what was going in here, yet more so to do with what was going out there with their woman on the street, that they no longer had any control over.*

In her letter she said she has missed me, and no man has ever filled the void I left in her heart, and she wants to come in and visit with me after all this time. Then the Captain let me know as I get closer to going home they are going put me back behind the gate for security reasons. I said ok. I was returned to the yard with three months left to go. I began to spend a lot more time around the brothers, praying and focusing on what parole is and what I need to do to get off of it. I continued to write Terri, she sent in a visiting form request and asked to come and see me. I thought about it for a while, then graciously declined. I have not heard from her since I sent that last outgoing letter.

The very last entry in my journal

01-11-03
"BISMILLAH IR RAHMAN IR RAHIM"

All praises are due to Allah! I have been blessed to witness another wonderful New Year dawn upon the long and arduous record on, or of mankind's existence. For me, this year (2003) is of very special significance because it is the very last one I will usher in from this venue, this setting. I've been gone from mainstream society for a very long time (8 years and four months). So much has occurred in my absence, so much has changed. **The winds of change oftentimes blow furiously about, scattering many things in their way.** Yet change is good nonetheless.

I, along with each and every one of my love ones are completely elated and consumed with my inevitable release on February 24th! I'm truly humbled by all of the attention and effort, all of the sacrifice and accommodations being made on my behalf. Yet more than ever, I realize that it is not about me. What all of this demonstrates is what our father reported to all of us, all of the time: **All of this represents the real beauty and power of Kinship, the very best in family ties and solidarity.**

I left this poem with the brothers on the yard:

"FOLLOW ALLAH OBEDIENTLY"

A lifestyle filled with vice and folly, totally incongruent, led me to bank robbery, on a bus to the State Pen I went.
Slammed in an environment where violence is the Golden Rule, with Gang members, Neo-Nazis, and so many other Fools!
Signs in two languages reminding us of no Warning Shots, if you get caught fighting you will be dropped on the spot!
Arrogant officers getting their jollies by stomping on our pride!
Cowards! If seen on the streets they'd just run and hide!
I've completed their disparaging orientation, tossed in a cold cell, nasty food, no phone calls or letters, man this is Hell!

> My cellie is stressing, Domestic Violence is his court case, that
> fool was brutal, he disfigured that sister's beautiful face!
> Am I dreaming? Physically here yet on the streets is my soul and
> heart, three children, women, now we're all apart!
> I'm down three months and already my dear relations are being
> taxed, my boys are rebelling and the women have just relaxed!
> I was the fool, so I repented and on my knees I remained for
> days, asking for forgiveness and help to change my ways!
> Now here I am, a living testament to **HIS LOVE,
> GRACE, AND MERCY**, the same invitation awaits
> you: **"FOLLOW ALLAH OBEDIENTLY!"**
> KBA

> "When all these blessings and curses *I* have set before you come
> on you and you take them to heart wherever the *LORD* your
> *GOD* disperses you among the nations, and when you and
> your children return to the *LORD* your *GOD* and you obey
> *HIM* with all your heart and soul according to everything
> *I* command you today, then the *LORD* your *GOD* will
> restore your fortunes and have compassion on you and gather
> you again from all the nations *HE* has scattered you."

Deuteronomy 30:1-3

There were so many spreads on the yard as my time grew near! My family, being who they are, sent me attire appropriate for a king, to walk out of the gate wearing, and my last week there, my father was heavy on my heart. I envisioned myself standing at his Tombstone in the cemetery. I prayed about it, and the very same night, my father came to visit with me. He needed to share these words with me before I was released: ***"BACADEE"***

"BACADEE"

It's been eight long trying years, since I was last at home, now I'm
standing in this cemetery, looking at your engraved Tombstone!
What an eerie experience this is for me, relating to
you in this way, I'm shaken by the thought of
it all, I really don't know what to say!
How I wish I had been there before you took your last breath; the
reigns you had on my life, became oh so evident in your death!
I went out and caught myself a felony case, wanted desperately by
the F.B.I.; your wise counsel to me, I chose to recklessly defy!
The Judge's gavel sealed my fate, sent away for a very long time,
throughout all of my trials in here, you were always on mind!
Just recalling your strong visage, gave me strength
to face the day, during those reflective moments, I could hear your voice say:
Kent, my son, what's done is done, you faced this responsibility,
I was disappointed in you, yet you're always very dear to me!
You know your mother and I taught you better than that,
yes indeed, I counseled you about those vices too, like alcohol and weed!
Yet men are truly wise but through experience, so from this you
must learn; discipline yourself again, in this you must be stern!
Turn your face toward **GOD** again in prayer, seek forgiveness and
change; remove bad habits and with good expand your range!
Soon this burden will be lifted from you, and you will be reunited
with the family; don't forget to visit my grave son,   *I love you:*

"BACADEE!"
KBA

"Great men stand like solitary towers in the city of GOD." "Lives of great men all around us, remind us that we can make our lives sublime, and departing, leave behind us some footprints on the sands of time."

HENRY WADSWORTH LONGFELLOW

ARTHUR DAVID BEAVERS JR., (BACADEE), 08/11/27-05/16/95

"In loving memory of my father's lifelong and life altering influence and dedication to his family"

The 24th of February, when I walked out of that package room, dressed in the finest civilian clothes money could buy and stepped out onto that yard to be escorted out of the prison, I was amazed and humbled at all of the attention it drew! All of the prison staff on the yard and all of the men on that yard were chanting, ***Akbar! Akbar! Akbar! Akbar!*** As I walked toward the gate they would have to let me out of, and I as I approached it, Tony, Dre, Mikal, Hakim, Lil Greg, were all standing by a Super stretch limousine, pearl white, cheering me on as I drew near, and I exited that gate, on that day, screaming: ***2, 594 days, 2,594 days! 2,594 days!***

The young Akbar at 19 years of age

"As I walked out the door toward my freedom, I knew that if I did not leave behind all the anger, hatred, and bitterness that I would still be in prison."

NELSON MANDELA

"Verily! **ALLAH** will not change the condition of a people until they change what is in their hearts."

QURAN 13:11

"As water reflects the face, so one's life reflects the heart."

PROVERBS 27:19

Epilogue

When I was released from prison in 2003, there were no programs then and there are still no programs in place today that are designed to help **inmates** that have been exposed to some of the most horrid experiences in life, (while incarcerated), transition back into society emotionally and mentally healthy. Albeit, our confinement being self-imposed, nonetheless, it is akin to **prisoners of war,** and just like **P.O.W.'s,** there should be periods of debriefing and evaluations with trained counselors and therapists upon release first, to ensure as best we can that people are being returned to society in a healthy state of mind, and if not they must undergo outpatient therapy and treatment. Present parole offices and parole officers don't offer any resources like this. (See the documentary on Netflix: **The Return**, released 2016)…

I saw first-hand throughout my experiences while incarcerated how the closing of and the lack of funding for Mental Health facilities in California placed these needy patients on the streets, and their untreated, dysfunctional behaviors inevitably led to contact with the police, and incarceration. **Many of them ending up in State prison demonstrating behaviors that said clearly they don't belong there.** Recent news worthy, yet very tragic cases: "A 34 year old woman rammed her car into barricades outside the White House with her infant child in the backseat." The Police believing it to be a terrorist attack, chased her down and shot her to death. **It** *was determined later that she had been struggling with mental illness for some time.*

"This came after a 34 year old man who had been complaining to his family and doctors that he was hearing voices and felt that people were out to get him walked into a Navy yard in Washington and gunned down twelve people." Now there are recent articles compiled by the **Federal government, Bureau of Prison Statistics, The Associated Press**, and the **Prison Policy Initiative**, that can be accessed instantly on the internet, which show clearly that there has been an explosion in the prison population since 2003, (more people locked up today than ever before), and the horrible conditions of overcrowding that are a direct result of this, aroused the avarice of fiendish capitalists and now *the* **privatization of prisons was born.**

So when States come under fire in the media now for the overcrowding of their facilities, they just bus **inmates** out to these **private prisons,** which is now *a billion dollar industry,* and some of the same companies and corporations we do business with every day in our homes are major shareholders. **Some of the same motivations that existed when the 13th Amendment was ratified in this country in 1865,** still exist today, **times ten!** (See the documentary on Netflix: **The 13th Amendment**, released October/2016)...The second largest slice of the incarceration pie in this country is local City and County jails, State prisons being the largest, (see recent article released in December/2016 by **Prison Policy Initiative**), *where millions of poor people in our inner cities are still being targeted, and arrested, having to come up with cash bails they don't have and because of this, having to remain in jail until some disposition is arrived at, which can take months.*

Today I walk more than I ever have, for two reasons, **health being the first,** and the other, **to get a firsthand account, a bird's eye view** of the real conditions in this bustling, beautiful Oceanside metropolis called Long Beach, where the diversity of people that reside here is so amazingly colorful. I have lived in Long Beach now for ten years. I'm originally from Atlanta, so whenever I'm home, I do the exact same thing, walk the neighborhoods.

As I take these walks, **my heart is impacted three times**! Cardiovascularly due to the exercise; emotionally due to the unprecedented number of homeless people I see on our streets today, (especially young people, women and children), and traumatically when I look around and observe how we have been *so desensitized to the tragic plight of our fellows...Going about our daily affairs as if these horrible conditions don't even exist!* The basic common-sense approach to fixing anything that is broken must begin with an earnest assessment of what really is wrong, and why? And it is evident by all of the broken people sprawled out all over our streets and sidewalks today, that this country's methods and systems which are supposed to enrich and protect its citizens, *are seriously broken!*

The old adage: *"Either you're a part of the solution or a part of the problem," reigns true today more than ever!* I, in good conscience, must be involved with other civic-minded people, institutions and communities that are determined to yield the kind of influence to affect constructive change in Congress, in our courts, in our prisons, and in law enforcement throughout this country, *so that someday justice really will be blind,* and all American citizens regardless of their socio-economic status or ethnicity, will always see justice being meted out fairly.

The alarming statistics about racial and ethnic disparity in the jails and prisons, and the alarming increase of incidents where unarmed African American men and women are being gunned down in our streets by the police *still says there is a major problem with race and justice in our country!* No longer should any of us informed citizens stand by in idle while injustice of any kind still reigns, and antiquated, ineffective laws and ordinances that promote the warehousing of people in these modern dungeons remains on the books, *as a superficial means of rehabilitation.*

We must rally together, and hold all of our elected officials accountable for challenging and eventually changing laws that don't safeguard and enrich the human experience in our families and communities. *We must see beyond our own self-interests*, and *recognize that this is a human condition,* that transcends race or gender, as evident by the homeless and prison populations today. In order for us to fix these problems and any others that can or will affect all of us, we must arrive at a place in our own hearts where we are genuinely ready to look at ourselves squarely and unflinchingly, *in that mirror,* and accept things for what they are, and not for what we hope them to be.

That we face these *barriers or walls* before us, (whatever they are, and wherever they be), with the courage and tenacity to make the kinds of necessary changes that are designed not to help just a few, *but the whole.* For we are one country under **GOD**, and united we stand and *divided we will fall!* In this Golden Age of highly sophisticated technology, *worldwide light!* Why would any of us want to linger in dark, Draconian practices when addressing these contemporary issues in our society?

"We cannot fix current problems with the same old solutions they were created under."

ALBERT EINSTEIN

If change isn't made, history becomes repetitious! Isn't the perennial theme of history struggle and progress? Do we idle in being a great country, or is the aim of its citizens to make this a greater country?

I proffer my people, African Americans to become a lot more proactive, and less reactive in our communities all across this country! Those of you in my peer group and older, that remember when there was a genuine caring in our communities, **and our communities really were villages that nurtured the child**, to come together like we have yet to, to preserve and articulate our history to our young people as only we can! For the greatest resource that any people have ever had is the youth in their ranks, and today, **there are real schisms between our youth and the older generations that must be bridged so that this very important work continues...**

This author purposefully extends three distinct perspectives in this book:

(1). His own unique experiences from his earliest memory; from one part of the country to the other, *spanning five decades,* which are accentuated by *creative writing*; *poetic verse,*

(2). The unique insights and perspectives of others, many of whom distinguished themselves as *icons*, leading thinkers of their time, in all of the *international quotations* strategically placed in this book, and,

(3). *An earnest, broken-down on your knees view,* of the **highest standards** mankind has ever been influenced or guided by in the placement of *scriptures* in this book, both **Quranic ayats and Biblical verses,** some of which illuminated the dark corridors my reckless wanderings led me down and brought me back into the full light and warmth of the sun once more, so that I may see clearly where I presently am, where I have been, and where it is I must now go; lending credence to and clarifying what it means to have *a real calling from GOD over one's life…*

Now in closing, last but certainly not least! I wrote on paper in prison, four chapters of this book, the introduction, some of the acknowledgements and dedication. Later on, I encountered a dynamic man known to us as Doc. He was a clerk that worked in the Lieutenant's office and he typed seventy words per minute. He agreed to begin typing this material for me in portions, he also assisted me with the original draft for the G.E.D. program at Tehachapi. He was a lifer and eventually, after a year or so, got moved back to Supermax. *Now this material was considered contraband, unlawful to have in your possession*

I had to hide those papers between stacks of legal court transcripts! When you consider all of the times my cell got turned upside down by officers at Tehachapi, then my transfer from there to C.M.C., then from there to the streets, *and all of the transitions I have been through from 2003 to 2017!!!* Which is another book and reading: **"BEYOND THEZE WALLZ TOO."** Due to be released in the summer or fall of 2018… (Smile)…

I have lost cars, trucks, storage units full of stuff, and the **LORD** preserved the original manuscripts, (handwritten copy and typed), the journal I kept while down, and my collection of poems that span more than forty years, written on paper so old they have turned different shades of brown, and that is truly amazing!!! ***ALL PRAISES BELONG***

TO GOD SOLELY!!! I experienced what I shared with you in this book, some of the graphic, horrific tragedies I purposefully forgot! In order to punch out the remaining six chapters and epilogue of this book I had to go back in time and think long and hard about some things. So I asked the **LORD** to allow me to relive them once more, so that I may be able to present them to all of you graphically! And now, in being transparent with all of you in this book, I have been blessed to tear down barriers or walls in my own life! ***Thank you....K. B. Akbar***

> "Success is to be measured not so much by the position one has reached in life, but by the obstacles which he had to overcome to get there."
>
> BOOKER T. WASHINGTON

"BEYOND THEZE WALLZ"

When we were born, we came into this world blank or empty, the things around us made impressions on you and me.

We did not choose our families, cities, or communities, yet these things shaped us all with very unique idiosyncrasies.

The way we talk, walk, our manners like thank you and please, the food that we like, no mayo, mustard, pickles and cheese.

If we were born into homes of hate, hate is what we see intently, if we were born into peace, peace we pursue relentlessly.

If we were born into dysfunction, molestation or abuse, this can last for generations if we don't decide to call a truce.

*If my grandfather was a pimp, or my mother was a prostitute,
this can go on forever if we are not given a better substitute.*

*Generations of men and women in and out of these prisons,
more time in there than out, creating major family schisms.*

*So with this poem I make a mass appeal to us all, let us do all
the work we must do to get* **"BEYOND THEZE WALLZ."**
KBA

A family photo that was long overdue, one that had not been taken in far more than a decade. (March/2003/Moreno Valley, Ca.). From top left to right: Tony, Deborah, Reginald, Gloria, June, and Me. Bottom left to right: Arthur, Momma, Andre and Angela. The Beavers Clan. (All smiles)!

About the Author

KENNETH BILAL AKBAR was born in 1958, at ole McClendon Hospital in downtown Atlanta. He is the sixth child of nine, spawned from the union of Gloria Shropshire Beavers and Arthur David Beavers Jr... Raised in Southwest Atlanta in a community called Joyland; he completed Elementary school at Thomas Heath Slater and High school at Luther Judson Price, where he was introduced to two of the loves of his life, (Annette and Poetry), and Mrs. Rawls, his English Literature teacher.

After spending a number of years in Public Safety, his marriage to Annette floundered, and he made his way out west to California, twenty-five years ago and hails Long Beach as his second home now. After spending the past thirteen years in EHS in the Oil and Gas Industry, where he has spent the last ten years in training, (training more than a half a million workers in workplace safety), he determined himself to get back to his passion for writing in 2016, and has other literary works that are forthcoming after this one. He writes under the ***nom de plumes of* K. B. Akbar and Halmicar Akbar**...

Made in the USA
Columbia, SC
03 July 2017